Eyewitness
Moon

Astronaut's food tray to
hold food packages down

Fossil coral

An image from the film
Voyage to the Moon

ROLL ALONG
PRAIRIE MOON

Popular American
song from 1935

Stamp commemorating
the Soviet Union's
Luna 3 spacecraft

Early German astronomer
Johannes Hevelius

Inuit Moon mask

Model of the
solar system

17th-century French
calendar for calculating
the Moon's phases

Eyewitness
Moon

NASA's Clementine
spacecraft

Written by
JACQUELINE MITTON

Geological map of the Moon

DK Publishing

Telescope used by Galileo

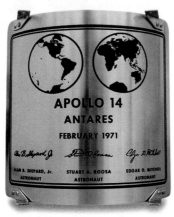

Apollo 14 mission plaque

Basalt Moon rock

DK

LONDON, NEW YORK, MUNICH,
MELBOURNE, AND DELHI

Consultant Dr. Ben Bussey

Senior editor Rob Houston
Senior art editor Alison Gardner
Managing editor Camilla Hallinan
Managing art editor Owen Peyton Jones
Art director Martin Wilson
Associate publisher Andrew Macintyre
Picture research Louise Thomas
Production editor Andy Hilliard
Senior production controller Pip Tinsley
Jacket designer Andy Smith
Jacket editor Adam Powley

DK DELHI

Senior editor Ankush Saikia
Designer Govind Mittal
DTP designer Preetam Singh
Editorial manager Glenda Fernandes
Design manager Romi Chakraborty
DTP coordinator Sunil Sharma

First published in the United States in 2009 by DK Publishing
375 Hudson Street, New York, New York 10014

Copyright © 2009 Dorling Kindersley Limited

09 10 11 12 13 10 9 8 7 6 5 4 3 2

ED744 – 12/08

A catalog record for this book is available
from the Library of Congress.

ISBN: 978 0 7566 4542 7 (HC)
978-0-7566-4543-4 (ALB)

Color reproduction by Colourscan, Singapore
Printed and bound by Toppan Printing Co. (Shenzen) Ltd., China

Discover more at

www.dk.com

Easter eggs

Lunar Prospector spacecraft

Lunokhod 1 unmanned lunar rover

Contents

Apollo 11 mission patch

Moon, myth, imagination

THE MOON IS THE BIGGEST and brightest heavenly body visible in the night sky and an influence on all our lives. We can be sure that our earliest ancestors observed it and wondered about it just as we do today. In many societies, the gods and goddesses of the Moon were among the most important deities and people invented myths about them. Thousands of years ago, the predecessors of today's astronomers made records of the Moon's position and learned how to predict its movement.

Ibis head

Human body

ANCIENT EGYPTIAN MOON GOD
Thoth was usually shown as a man with the head of an ibis (a water bird). Often, he wears a moon headdress. The Egyptians said he invented writing and made the calculations to form the heavens, stars, and Earth. Later, the ancient Greeks credited him with inventing astronomy and other sciences.

THE ZIGGURAT AT UR
One of the earliest records of Moon worship is found in Mesopotamia, in present-day Iraq. More than 4,000 years ago, the people of the city of Ur built a giant temple of mud bricks, called a ziggurat. Here, they worshiped their Moon god, Nanna. Some 1,500 years later, people of a new civilization called the Babylonians used this same temple to honor their own Moon god, Sin.

Ziggurat stood about 65 ft (20 m) high

Shrine

Platform

Base measured 207 ft (63 m) by 141 ft (43 m)

Ceremonial steps

ROMAN MOON GODDESS
In ancient Rome, the goddess Luna was associated with the Moon's light. She is often pictured with a crescent Moon on her head. Since she is also known as the bringer of light, she is shown carrying a torch in her hand. The word "lunar" comes from her name, which is Latin for "Moon."

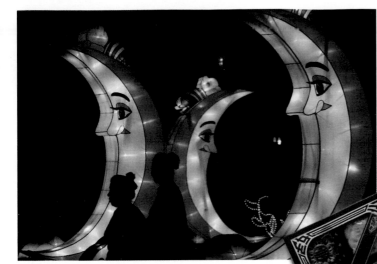

CHINESE MOON FESTIVAL
Every fall, Chinese people around the world celebrate the Moon Festival at full Moon in the eighth lunar month. They carry bright lanterns and watch the Moon rise. Mooncakes are the traditional festival food. They are a kind of rich, sweet pastry, sometimes with a cooked egg yolk inside to represent the Moon.

Mooncakes

Feathers represent stars

Hoops symbolize the heavens

White area represents air

MOON SPIRIT
This 19th-century mask was carved by the Inuit people of Alaska. It depicts Tarqeq, the spirit of the Moon, and it would have been used in ceremonial dances. Inuit folklore includes many stories about Tarqeq. He was believed to be a great hunter who watched over the behavior of humans from the sky.

CARVED AZTEC STONE
This ancient stone from Mexico City was carved by the Aztec people, before Europeans arrived in the Americas. It depicts the myth of the Moon goddess Coyolxauhqui. She was killed by her brother, who cut her body into pieces and threw her head up into the sky, where it became the Moon.

WEREWOLVES AND THE MOON
The myth of humans that change shape into bloodthirsty wolves was popular in Medieval Europe, where the wolf was the most feared wild animal. In his book of folklore completed in 1214 CE, the writer Gervase of Tilbury said the transformation of these so-called werewolves was believed to be triggered by a full Moon.

STONEHENGE
Stonehenge in southern England was built by Stone Age people between 3000 and 2000 BCE. No one is sure of its true purpose, but scientists who have studied the alignment of the stones suspect they may have been used to observe the Sun and Moon, and to predict eclipses (see page 14).

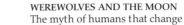

Earth's partner

Full Moon

Rabbit or hare

Man

Hunter

Woman

THE MOON IS OUR NEAREST neighbor in space and a familiar object in the sky, sometimes visible by day as well as at night. Measuring 2,160 miles (3,476 km) in diameter, it is our natural satellite—another world orbiting our planet—but it is very different. Earth, with its air and liquid water, supports a multitude of life-forms. It is also an active planet with moving continents and is frequently rocked by violent earthquakes and volcanoes. By contrast, the lifeless, airless Moon is a dry, hostile place, where little ever changes. Its surface has remained much the same for about 3 billion years. Although the Moon is a ball of dark gray rock, it reflects the light of the Sun and it appears clear and bright to us. It is the only object in space whose surface features can be seen by the naked eye from Earth.

CONTRAST IN ATMOSPHERE
Though the Moon and Earth are neighbors, they are very different. Earth's gravity is strong enough to hold on to a thick layer of air, where clouds can form and blanket large areas of the globe. By contrast, the Moon's gravity is only one-sixth of the Earth's. It keeps hold of only a very thin atmosphere—so thin that it is invisible and would fit inside a jam jar.

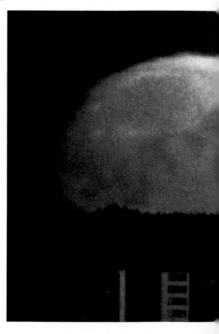

ARTISTIC INSPIRATION
The Moon has inspired countless artists, poets, and musicians of all kinds. The popular song *Roll Along Prairie Moon* was written in 1935. The lyrics were by the American songwriter Harry MacPherson. At the time, cowboys would drive herds of cattle across the wide, grassy plains of the American prairies. In this song a lonely cowboy sings about his lady love to the Moon above the prairie.

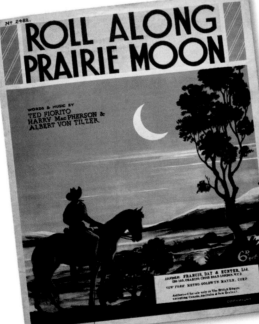

A cowboy gazes at the Moon

PATTERNS ON THE MOON
To many people, the patterns made by the light and dark areas on the Moon suggest familiar shapes. They are best seen when the Moon is full or nearly full. In the West, people mostly see the face of a man, but in the East people more often refer to the rabbit or hare in the Moon.

A WORLD IN THE MOON
Until the 17th century, most people thought that the Moon must be a smooth, mirrorlike sphere. They believed that the markings they could see were reflections of seas and continents on Earth. Writers such as the English clergyman John Wilkins argued that the dark and light areas were sea and land and that the Moon could be inhabited. Wilkins, a founding member of the Royal Society, published his ideas in 1638 in a book called *The Discovery of a World in the Moone*.

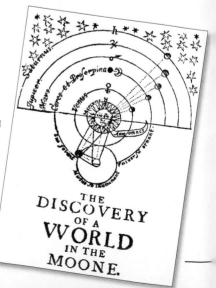

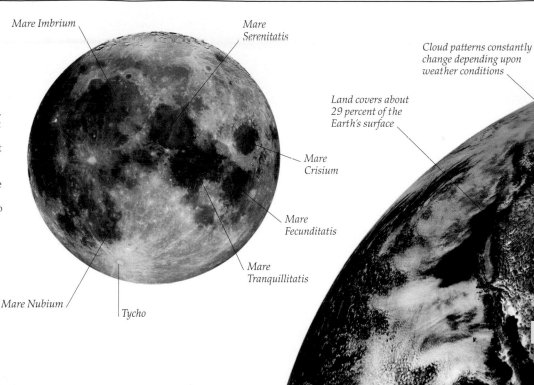

Mare Imbrium

Mare Serenitatis

Mare Crisium

Mare Fecunditatis

Mare Tranquillitatis

Tycho

Mare Nubium

Cloud patterns constantly change depending upon weather conditions

Land covers about 29 percent of the Earth's surface

NAKED-EYE MOON
The main features on the Moon are visible even without a telescope. The large dark areas are easy to spot and have "watery" names, dating from the time when people thought they were seas. Many of these are called *mare*—plural *maria*—which is Latin for "sea." Several of the large craters or depressions are also easy to see, especially at full Moon. Tycho is the most prominent crater and its rays make the Moon look like a silvery fruit.

THE BLUE PLANET
Earth is nearly four times bigger than the Moon. Liquid water flows on Earth's surface because we have the right combination of pressure and temperature beneath our thick layer of air. Any water on the Moon would evaporate into space, although ice may have survived at the bottom of deep craters near the poles. With no water and almost no atmosphere, the Moon has never had wind, rain, oceans, or rivers to shape its landscape.

MOON ON THE HORIZON
When the Moon is rising or setting, it often appears a reddish color and its shape can be squashed and distorted. This is because we are viewing the Moon by looking not straight up, but sideways through thousands of miles of atmosphere, which bends and distorts the light. The Moon also looks larger near the horizon, but that is an optical illusion. The actual size of the Moon does not change as it rises, but no one has been able to explain why it seems to do so.

RING AROUND THE MOON
The full Moon is sometimes surrounded by a ghostly ring or halo of light, particularly in winter. A halo appears when the Moon is seen through a thin, cold layer of cloud and rays of moonlight are bent through falling ice crystals.

Oceans cover about 71 percent of the Earth's surface

Earth's atmosphere extends up to 75 miles (120 km) above its surface, gradually thinning out into space

A waltz in space

THE MOON SWINGS AROUND EARTH like a dance partner. Its orbit or path is not quite circular but elongated into an ellipse, with the Earth off center. The average distance between the Moon and Earth is about 238,900 miles (384,400 km). A car traveling at 60 mph (100 kph) would take around 160 days to go that far. Over one circuit, we see the Moon's visible shape change from a thin crescent to full and back again. These changes in shape are called phases, and the cycle of phases takes about a month. The times of moonrise and moonset also change during the Moon's phases.

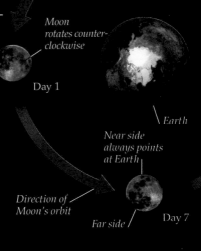

Moon rotates counter-clockwise

Day 1

Earth

Near side always points at Earth

Direction of Moon's orbit

Far side Day 7

ROTATION OF THE MOON
On each orbit around Earth, the Moon also turns once on its axis, so it always keeps the same face toward Earth. The opposite side always faces away and is called the far side. Due to its slow rotation matching its orbit, a day on the Moon lasts the same time as a month on Earth.

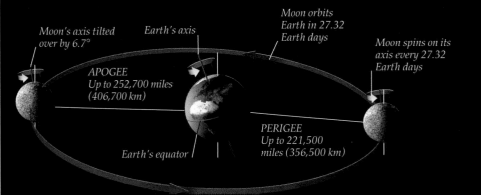

Moon's axis tilted over by 6.7°   *Earth's axis*   *Moon orbits Earth in 27.32 Earth days*

APOGEE Up to 252,700 miles (406,700 km)

Moon spins on its axis every 27.32 Earth days

Earth's equator

PERIGEE Up to 221,500 miles (356,500 km)

THE MOON'S ORBIT
This diagram shows the Moon making one orbit around Earth. In fact, its path changes slightly on every circuit and only repeats every 18.6 years. The nearest and farthest points of one circuit are called the perigee and apogee.

View of the Moon from Earth

8. CRESCENT
Only a thin sliver is visible. The Moon has nearly waned.

Sunlight

1. NEW MOON
The Moon's far side points toward the Sun. The near side is in darkness and cannot be seen from Earth.

View of the Moon from space

2. CRESCENT
The Moon is said to be waxing, or growing. Part of the near side becomes visible from Earth.

SPOT THE DIFFERENCE
The area of the Moon facing Earth varies slightly. The difference is shaded in pink here. During one cycle of phases, we see not half of the Moon's surface, but 59 percent. This variation, called libration, is mainly due to the elliptical shape of the Moon's orbit and the small tilt of the Moon's axis of spin.

PHASES OF THE MOON
The Moon shines by reflecting sunlight, so only the side of the Moon facing the Sun is illuminated. Over the course of the Moon's monthly orbit, all parts of it, including the far side, move into sunlight at some time. From Earth we see different amounts of the near side illuminated according to how far the Moon has traveled on its orbit. The pictures around the outside of this diagram show the Moon's phase—how it appears from Earth—at different points of its orbit.

LASER RANGING
The precise distance to the Moon from Earth can be measured to a few millimeters by firing a powerful laser from a telescope and timing how long it takes for the light to be reflected back. The laser beam is aimed at reflectors placed on the Moon by Apollo astronauts and a Soviet robotic rover. On average, the beam takes about 2.6 seconds to travel to the Moon and back.

Saturn

LUNAR OCCULTATION
The Moon is nearer to us than any planet, asteroid, or star, so it often hides—or occults—one of them. This picture shows an occultation of the planet Saturn. Timing when objects disappear and reappear at the start and end of occultations helps astronomers to track the Moon's motion accurately.

7. LAST QUARTER
Half of the Moon's near side is visible. A quarter of the cycle remains.

6. GIBBOUS
The Moon is said to be waning or shrinking.

Earth

5. FULL MOON
The Moon's near side faces directly toward the Sun.

CHANGING SIZE
The Moon's distance from Earth varies by about 30,000 miles (50,000 km). The nearer it is the larger it looks. At its closest, the Moon appears about 14 percent bigger than when it is at its greatest distance. It also shines about 30 percent more brightly.

The Moon's orbit

3. FIRST QUARTER
The Moon has completed a quarter of its orbit. Half of the Moon's near side is visible from Earth.

4. GIBBOUS
The Moon is said to be waxing gibbous.

SUNSET CRESCENT
The time when the Moon rises and sets varies with its phase. For instance, a crescent Moon is never seen in the middle of the night, but only in the eastern sky just before dawn or in the western sky around sunset.

The Moon's calendar

THE COMMON CALENDAR that we use to order
our lives is based on the yearly orbit of Earth
around the Sun, which gives us our seasons,
and on Earth's daily rotation, which
gives us day and night. But the division
of a year into months comes from the
Moon's orbit. The time between two
new moons is called a synodic month,
from a Greek word for "meeting." Many
cultures have used calendars based on
12 synodic months in a year. But unless
extra days are added each year, these lunar
calendars are soon out of step with the
seasons. However, they are still widely used
for setting the dates of religious observances.

ASTRONOMICAL CLOCK
Astronomical clocks mark the passage of days,
months, and years. This one, at the Old Town Hall
in Prague, dates from 1410. The top dial has three
pointers and represents the motion of the Sun,
Moon, and stars around Earth. The lower dial is a
calendar showing the months of the year.

Moon pointer

*Inner dial shows sky
divided into 12 signs
of the zodiac*

*Background shows
day, twilight,
and night*

*Outer dial is a
24-hour clock*

*Illustrations
for months
of the year*

*Wheel turns for
Moon's phase*

THE 19-YEAR CYCLE
Twelve lunar months add up to only 354 days—11 days
short of a full year. However, 19 years is almost exactly
235 lunar months. People who used lunar calendars could
add seven extra months every 19 years to keep in step
with the seasons. This French calendar from 1680 includes
a table and two wheels. It calculates the Moon's phases
over a 19-year cycle and also shows the days of the week.

SYNODIC AND SIDEREAL MONTHS

Circling around the sky, the Moon returns to the same position after 27.32 days. This period is called a sidereal month from a Latin word meaning "star" or "constellation." During that time, Earth has moved along its orbit around the Sun, so the Moon needs more time to complete all its phases. This takes a synodic month, which lasts 29.54 days.

Earth

Moon begins orbit

Earth's orbit

Moon completes orbit one sidereal month later

Moon completes phases one synodic month later

Sun

Maror (bitter herb—horseradish)

Zeroa (lamb shank bone)

Charoset (apple, nut, spice, and wine)

Beitzah (egg)

Karpas (vegetable or parsley)

Chazeret (bitter vegetable—lettuce)

JEWISH PASSOVER

The dates of Jewish religious festivals are set according to a historic lunar calendar and their dates in the common calendar vary from year to year. The celebration of Passover, for example, starts on the 15th day of the Jewish month of *Nissan*. At Passover, families eat a special ritual meal of five or six symbolic foods, called the *seder*.

Traditional painted Easter egg

EASTER TIME

The date of the Christian festival of Easter was originally the first Sunday after a particular full Moon. Today, the date is set by reading tables that simplify the cycles of the Moon rather than the date of a real full Moon. Eastern and Western churches often celebrate Easter on different dates because they use different calendars.

THE MOON AND ISLAM

The religious Islamic calendar is based on lunar months. Because 12 lunar months take only about 354 days, Islamic holy days fall 10 or 11 days earlier each year by the common calendar. The symbol of the crescent Moon is often linked with Islam. The link began when the Muslim founders of the Ottoman Empire conquered the city of Constantinople (present-day Istanbul) in 1453 and adopted the city's emblem—the crescent Moon—as their own.

Crescent moon on the East London Mosque in the UK

Minaret, from which the voice of the muezzin calls Muslims to prayer

Dome of the mosque

NEW LUNAR MONTH

The first sighting of the slim crescent Moon, appearing just 30 hours after the new Moon, marks the start of each month in the Islamic lunar calendar. Ramadan, the important month of fasting observed by Muslims, begins at the start of the ninth lunar month. It marks the time that the first verse of the Qur'an was revealed to Muhammad and finishes with a feast at the next new Moon.

Eclipses

PEOPLE TRAVEL ALL OVER the world to experience a total solar eclipse. During this dramatic natural phenomenon, the Moon blocks out the Sun's light. Sometimes, the Moon itself goes into an eclipse, taking on a mysterious coppery hue. The Moon, Sun, and Earth do not line up to create an eclipse every month. At least two solar eclipses happen every year, though most are partial. Up to seven lunar and solar eclipses can fall in a year. The pattern of eclipses repeats on a cycle of 6,585.32 days (about 18 years).

ECLIPSE OF THE MOON
Lunar eclipses take place only at full Moon. During a total eclipse, Earth gradually moves between the Moon and the Sun. Earth's shadow seems to creep across the Moon's surface. Even when totally eclipsed, the Moon remains dimly lit by red light, which is sunlight reaching the Moon after it has been bent and scattered through the edge of Earth's atmosphere. The period of totality can last up to 1 hour 47 minutes.

Moon being eclipsed

Christopher Columbus

COLUMBUS'S ECLIPSE
In the past, eclipses were feared or regarded as portents of evil. In 1504, the Spanish explorer Christopher Columbus became stranded with his crew in Jamaica. He knew that there would be a total eclipse of the Moon on February 29 and used this to scare the local Arawak people. He told them that the Moon was being taken away and would be restored only if they helped him. The trick worked and Columbus and his crew were later rescued.

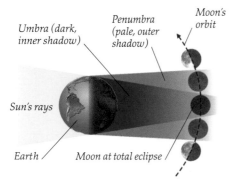

Umbra (dark, inner shadow)

Penumbra (pale, outer shadow)

Moon's orbit

Sun's rays

Earth

Moon at total eclipse

LUNAR ECLIPSE
For an eclipse of the Moon to take place, the Sun, Earth, and Moon must line up at full Moon. Lunar eclipses occur when the Moon passes through Earth's shadow. They can be seen from any location where the Moon has risen before the eclipse.

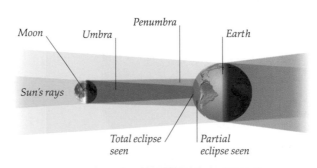

Moon

Umbra

Penumbra

Earth

Sun's rays

Total eclipse seen

Partial eclipse seen

SOLAR ECLIPSE
A solar eclipse is seen when a new Moon crosses in front of the Sun and casts a shadow on part of Earth's surface. Total eclipses of the Sun are seen only over a narrow area, because the Moon's shadow is small when it reaches Earth. Observers in a region outside this area of totality see only a partial eclipse.

ANCIENT ECLIPSE RECORDS

Eclipses have been recorded for thousands of years. Inscribed Chinese oracle bones like this one mention eclipses in around 1300 BCE. The earliest reference in recorded history concerns two Chinese court astrologers who were beheaded for failing to predict a solar eclipse in 2134 BCE.

Inscribed characters

SOLAR PROMINENCES

When the brilliant disk of the Sun is hidden by the Moon during a total eclipse, it is sometimes possible to see solar prominences at the Sun's edge. These huge tongues of hot gas surge out into space from the Sun. The prominence shown here was recorded during the eclipse of July 11, 1991.

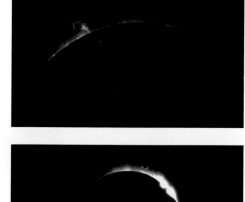

BAILY'S BEADS

The edge of the Moon is uneven because of its mountains and valleys. At the beginning and end of a total solar eclipse, sunlight often bursts through several valleys. The effect is called Baily's Beads, after the English astronomer Francis Baily (1774–1844).

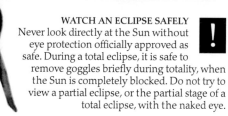

Arawak people fear the eclipse

WATCH AN ECLIPSE SAFELY

Never look directly at the Sun without eye protection officially approved as safe. During a total eclipse, it is safe to remove goggles briefly during totality, when the Sun is completely blocked. Do not try to view a partial eclipse, or the partial stage of a total eclipse, with the naked eye.

TOTAL SOLAR ECLIPSE

As the partial phase of a total solar eclipse progresses, the Moon gradually covers the Sun. The moment of totality comes when the Sun's yellow disk is completely hidden. The sky goes dark and it is possible to see the Sun's corona (faint outer layers of gas) extending out from the Sun like a white halo. Totalities can last up to 7.5 minutes, but they are mostly much shorter. This eclipse in July 1991 was nearly 7 minutes long. Images taken at different stages of the eclipse have been put together to make this picture.

PARTIAL SOLAR ECLIPSE

When the Moon and Sun are not perfectly aligned, an eclipse of the Sun may be only partial, as seen here in India in March 2007. Observers also experience a partial eclipse if they look at a total eclipse from outside the area of totality.

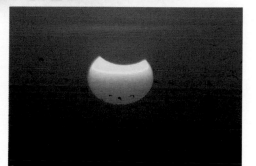

ANNULAR ECLIPSE

The Moon and Sun appear to be nearly the same size in our sky but both vary slightly (see page 11). An annular (ring-shaped) eclipse occurs when the Moon crosses directly in front of the Sun and its apparent size happens to be less than the Sun's. This one was seen in January 1992.

Tides

THE EBB AND FLOW OF tides around the world's coasts are daily reminders of the Moon's influence on our planet. The Moon's gravity pulling on Earth is the principal cause of ocean tides. It distorts Earth's rocky ball by just an inch or so but stretches the oceans by around 3–10 ft (1–3 m). The constant drag of tides is slowing Earth's rotation and causing the Moon's orbit to widen. Days are lengthening by about 2 milliseconds per century and the Moon moves about 1½ in (3.8 cm) farther away each year.

High tide near St. Abbs Harbour, Scotland

Low tide near St. Abbs Harbour, Scotland

Tidal bulge forms here because the Moon's gravity pulls Earth's center more than Earth's far side

Earth's orbit

Earth

Water forms a tidal bulge

Moon's gravity pulls Earth's oceans

Moon

Each coastal place experiences a high tide as the tidal bulge moves past

Earth's spin

Low tides occur on either side of tidal bulges

Tidal bulge is ahead of the Moon

Moon's orbit

TIDES AND THE MOON
The Moon's gravity stretches Earth into a slightly oval shape because its pull is strongest on the side of Earth facing the Moon and weakest on the opposite side. The oceans stretch more than the rocky ball of Earth because they are liquid. This makes tidal bulges form on both sides of the globe. The daily rotation of Earth drags the tidal bulges with it so they sweep around the world slightly ahead of the Moon rather than directly in line with it.

HIGH AND LOW TIDE
The height and pattern of tides can vary from coast to coast as a result of many different factors, such as the shape of the coastline, and the depth of water. The difference between high and low tide in the narrow, curving Bay of Fundy in Canada is nearly 53 ft (16 m), the greatest range in the world. Most coasts have two tides a day, 12 hours 25 minutes apart, but some have only one every 24 hours 50 minutes.

TIDAL POWER STATION
The power of tides can be harnessed to generate electricity. This tidal power plant, which opened in Brittany, France, in 1966, was the first in the world. A barrage 2,461 ft (750 m) long spans the estuary of the Rance river. Water flows through turbines when the tide comes in and goes out. The water turns the turbines, generating electricity.

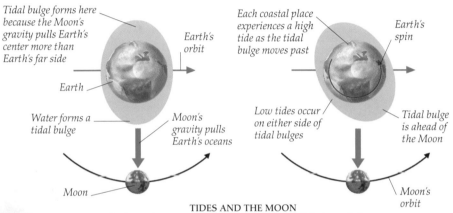

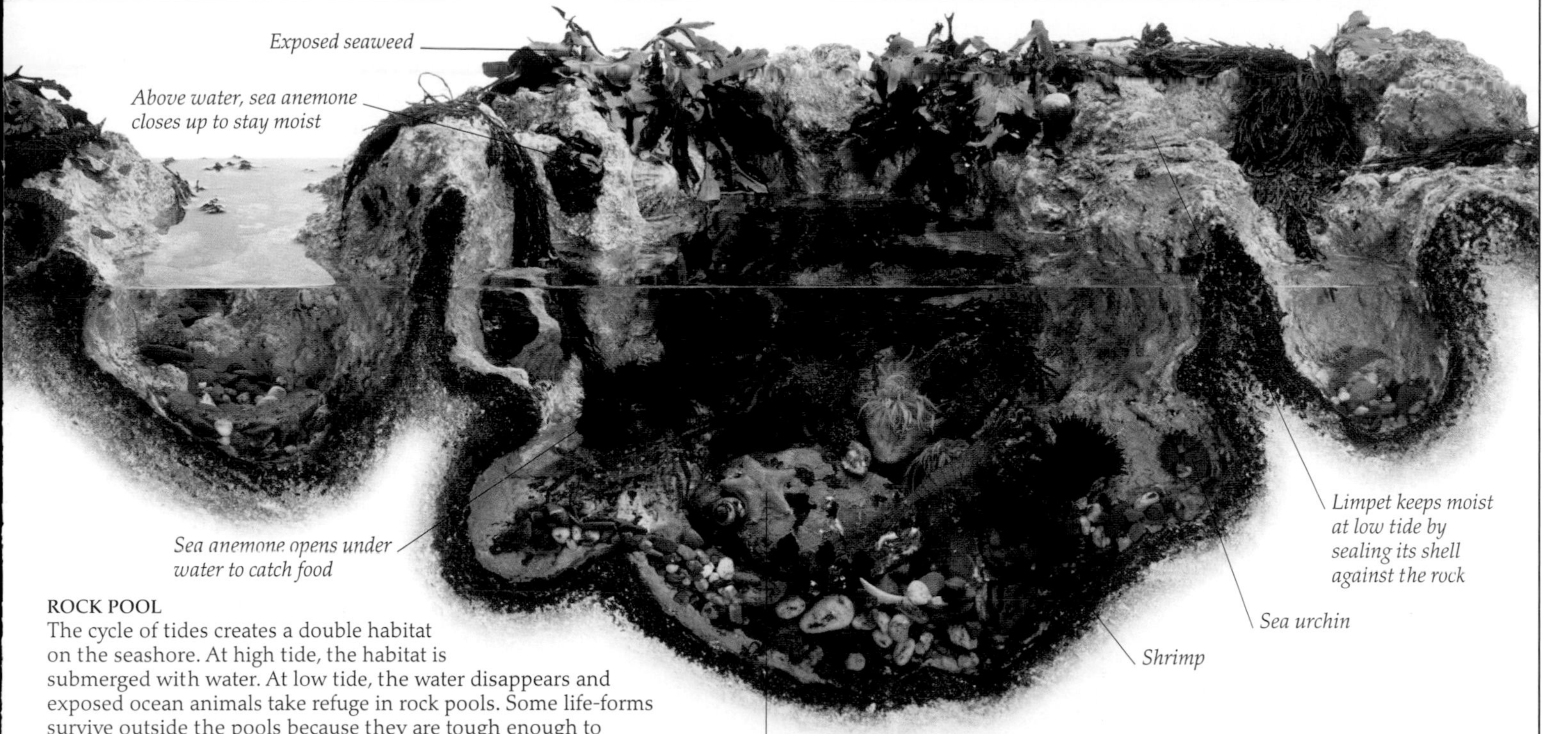

Exposed seaweed

Above water, sea anemone closes up to stay moist

Limpet keeps moist at low tide by sealing its shell against the rock

Sea urchin

Shrimp

Sea anemone opens under water to catch food

ROCK POOL
The cycle of tides creates a double habitat on the seashore. At high tide, the habitat is submerged with water. At low tide, the water disappears and exposed ocean animals take refuge in rock pools. Some life-forms survive outside the pools because they are tough enough to tolerate drying out. This pool is shown at low tide.

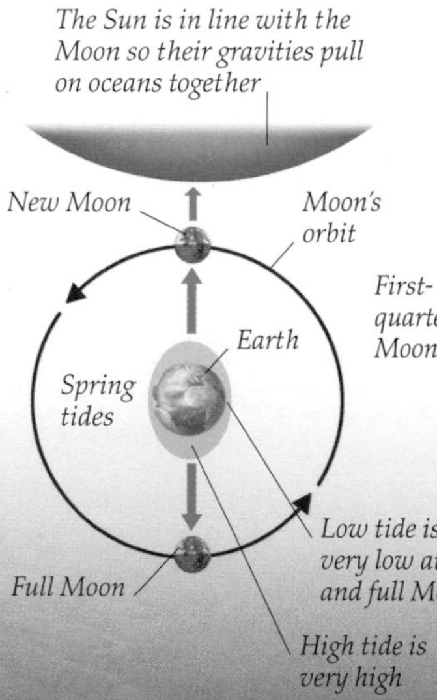

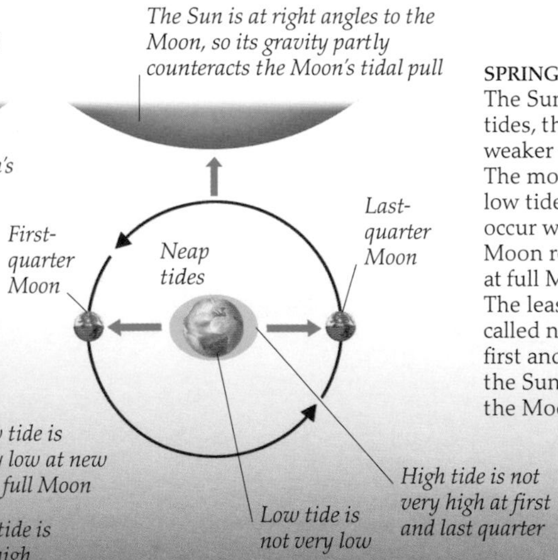

Sea star

The Sun is in line with the Moon so their gravities pull on oceans together

The Sun is at right angles to the Moon, so its gravity partly counteracts the Moon's tidal pull

New Moon

Moon's orbit

First-quarter Moon

Last-quarter Moon

Earth

Neap tides

Spring tides

Full Moon

Low tide is very low at new and full Moon

Low tide is not very low

High tide is not very high at first and last quarter

High tide is very high

SPRING AND NEAP TIDES
The Sun also affects ocean tides, though its pull is weaker than the Moon's. The most extremely high and low tides, called spring tides, occur when the Sun and Moon reinforce each other at full Moon and new Moon. The least extreme tides, called neap tides, happen at first and last quarter, when the Sun's pull partly opposes the Moon's gravity.

Fine growth bands in base

LONGER DAYS
Some corals have daily growth bands, like yearly tree rings. Counting growth bands in fossil corals from different periods shows that day length was shorter in the past—about 22 hours 300 million years ago, and about 21 hours 500 million years ago.

Birth of the Moon

THE MOON AND EARTH ARE unusual in the solar system, because they exist as a pair of worlds of very similar size. Scientists have puzzled for centuries about how Earth acquired such a large partner. Before the Apollo Moon missions, there were three main theories. One was that the Moon and Earth formed together as a double planet. Others suggested that the Moon was spun off by a rapidly spinning Earth, perhaps from where the Pacific Ocean is now. Alternatively, the Moon might have been a stray body, captured by Earth's gravity. The Apollo missions were expected to settle which theory was correct but none of their findings fit the facts. There had to be a different explanation.

1. Sun forms in a nebula (a cloud of dust and gas)

2. Cloud begins spinning and forms a disk

3. Small planetesimals form

4. Planets form from planetesimals

BIRTH OF THE SOLAR SYSTEM
Most planetary scientists think that the planets and other bodies in the solar system formed about 4.6 billion years ago within a rotating disk of dust and gas surrounding the newly born Sun. Clumps called planetesimals gradually came together in a process called accretion, but there were also high speed collisions that broke some clumps apart again. Small pieces that were left over became comets and asteroids.

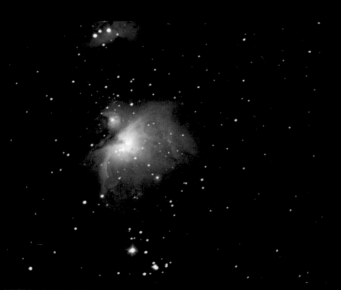

NEBULAR THEORY
Stars and their planetary systems are born in nebulae like this one, the Orion Nebula. One theory of the Moon's origin suggested that it and Earth condensed out of the nebula surrounding the Sun. But this idea cannot explain the differences between Moon rocks and Earth rocks and why the Moon's iron core is very small.

GIANT COLLISION
A giant collision between the newly formed Earth and a small planet about the size of Mars is now the most popular explanation for how Earth acquired its Moon. This theory explains better than any other the structure, composition, and orbit of the Moon. Computer simulations can show how it probably happened.

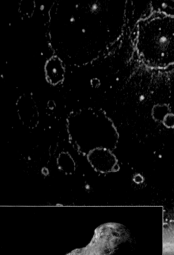

1 GLANCING COLLISION
About 4.55 billion years ago, when Earth was only 50 million years old, a smaller planet had formed in a nearby orbit and the two were on a collision course. At this time, the solar system was a violent place where major collisions were not uncommon. The impact with Earth was not head-on but its cataclysmic force blasted enormous amounts of rock from both planets as a white hot vapor. This was the material from which the Moon would form. The very high temperatures it reached can explain why the Moon has more of certain chemical elements than Earth, and less of others.

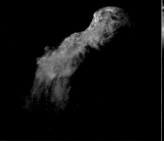

2 HOT CLOUD
Just hours after the impact, vast clouds of hot gas and dust and fragments of rock were streaming away from Earth. Some traveled fast enough to escape Earth's gravity.

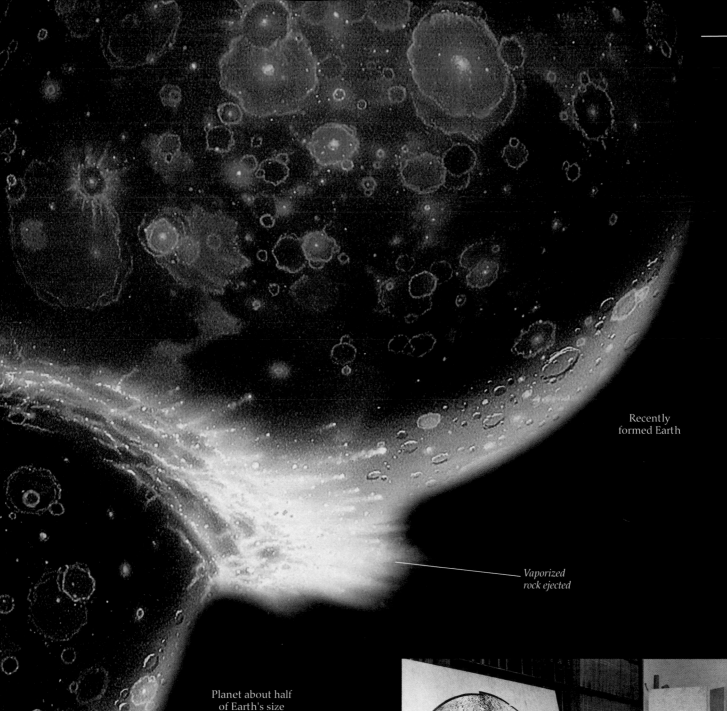

Recently
formed Earth

Vaporized
rock ejected

Planet about half
of Earth's size

3 RING OF DEBRIS
Some of the ejected gas, rock, and dust remained captured in orbit around Earth. It cooled rapidly and, soon after the collision, the circling cloud collapsed into a ring of debris.

4 FORMATION OF MOON
Within only a few years, material in the circulating ring began to clump together. Pieces of rock were attracted to one another by gravity and eventually formed the Moon.

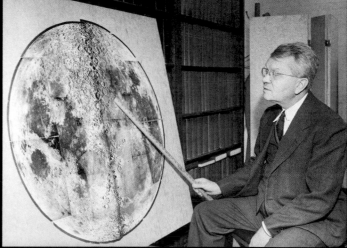

HAROLD C. UREY
The American scientist Harold C. Urey (1893–1981) received the Nobel Prize for chemistry in 1934 and started to study the Moon in the 1940s. He favored the theory that the Moon originally formed elsewhere in the solar system and was captured by Earth 4.5 billion years ago. Urey was probably wrong about that, but he wanted to see humans land on the Moon and his enthusiasm influenced NASA's early space program.

The Moon takes shape

THE MOON AS WE SEE IT TODAY was mostly shaped billions of years ago, when its volcanoes erupted with lava, and comets, asteroids, and meteoroids pounded its surface. The first crust to crystalize on the newly formed Moon was soon a mass of impact craters. Later, there were fewer large collisions, and the low-lying basins created by the largest impacts flooded with lava that solidified into dark gray plains.

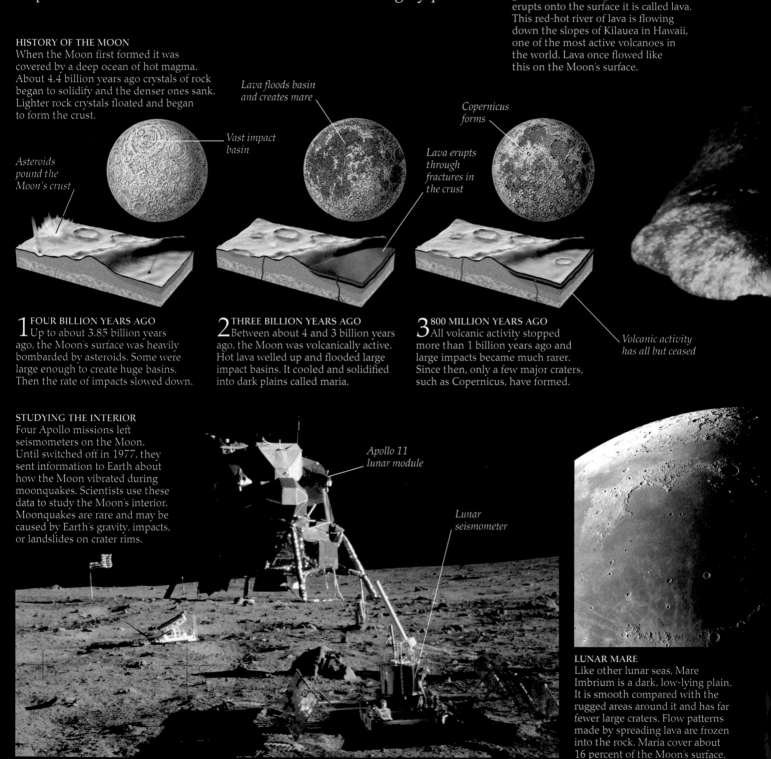

LAVA FLOW
Hot molten rock under ground is called magma. When it erupts onto the surface it is called lava. This red-hot river of lava is flowing down the slopes of Kilauea in Hawaii, one of the most active volcanoes in the world. Lava once flowed like this on the Moon's surface.

HISTORY OF THE MOON
When the Moon first formed it was covered by a deep ocean of hot magma. About 4.4 billion years ago crystals of rock began to solidify and the denser ones sank. Lighter rock crystals floated and began to form the crust.

Lava floods basin and creates mare

Vast impact basin

Copernicus forms

Asteroids pound the Moon's crust

Lava erupts through fractures in the crust

Volcanic activity has all but ceased

1 FOUR BILLION YEARS AGO
Up to about 3.85 billion years ago, the Moon's surface was heavily bombarded by asteroids. Some were large enough to create huge basins. Then the rate of impacts slowed down.

2 THREE BILLION YEARS AGO
Between about 4 and 3 billion years ago, the Moon was volcanically active. Hot lava welled up and flooded large impact basins. It cooled and solidified into dark plains called maria.

3 800 MILLION YEARS AGO
All volcanic activity stopped more than 1 billion years ago and large impacts became much rarer. Since then, only a few major craters, such as Copernicus, have formed.

STUDYING THE INTERIOR
Four Apollo missions left seismometers on the Moon. Until switched off in 1977, they sent information to Earth about how the Moon vibrated during moonquakes. Scientists use these data to study the Moon's interior. Moonquakes are rare and may be caused by Earth's gravity, impacts, or landslides on crater rims.

Apollo 11 lunar module

Lunar seismometer

LUNAR MARE
Like other lunar seas, Mare Imbrium is a dark, low-lying plain. It is smooth compared with the rugged areas around it and has far fewer large craters. Flow patterns made by spreading lava are frozen into the rock. Maria cover about 16 percent of the Moon's surface.

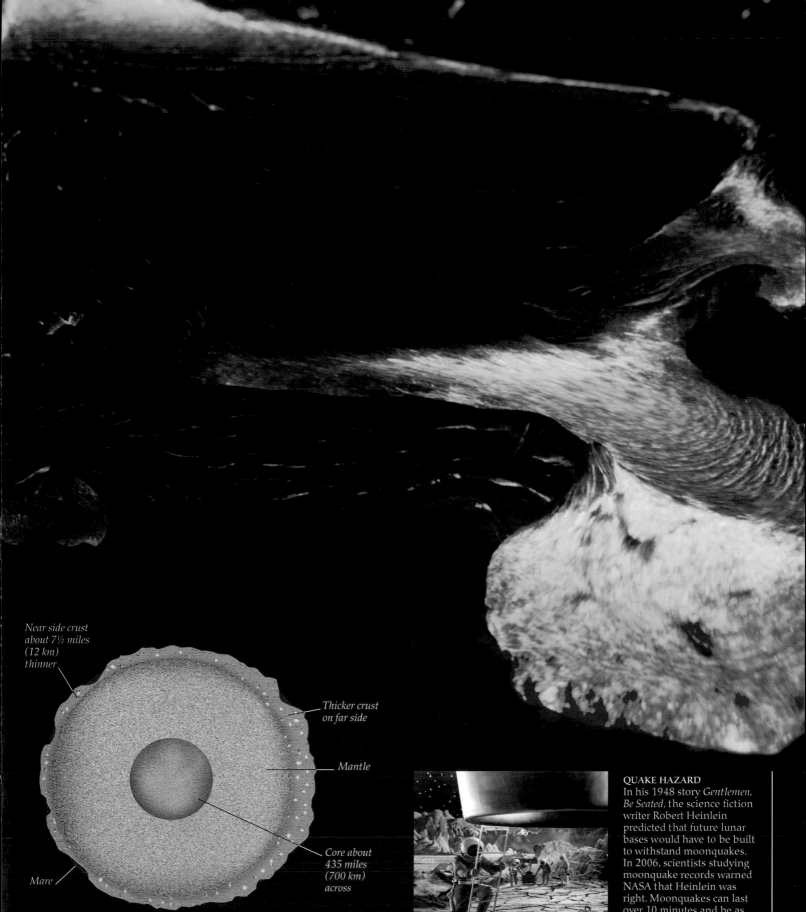

Near side crust
about 7½ miles
(12 km)
thinner

Thicker crust
on far side

Mantle

Core about
435 miles
(700 km)
across

Mare

STRUCTURE OF THE MOON

The interior of the Moon is layered but we are not certain about its
structure. The outer crust is 12–75 miles (20–120 km) thick but
the near side is thinner on average. More maria formed in the near
side, possibly because lava reached the surface more easily through
the thinner crust. The crust lies over a deep mantle of denser rock.
The small core is mainly iron and may be partly molten.

QUAKE HAZARD

In his 1948 story *Gentlemen,
Be Seated*, the science fiction
writer Robert Heinlein
predicted that future lunar
bases would have to be built
to withstand moonquakes.
In 2006, scientists studying
moonquake records warned
NASA that Heinlein was
right. Moonquakes can last
over 10 minutes and be as
strong as earthquakes that
cause damage to buildings.
Shown here is a scene from
the popular 1950 movie
Destination Moon, whose
screenplay was cowritten
by Heinlein.

The Moon's surface

THE LUNAR LANDSCAPE IS STARK and colorless. Every part is covered with a thick layer of powdery gray dust and scattered with boulders. Craters large and small pit the entire surface. Huge basins filled with lava are ringed with mountains. The plains of solidified lava in the basins reveal their volcanic origin with a variety of features such as pitted domes, collapsed lava tubes, winding cliffs, and humpy ridges. For astronauts, the airless environment is harsh. During the day the temperature at the equator soars as high as 240°F (120°C) only to plummet to -270°F(-170°C) at night, and there is no protection from the Sun's dangerous radiation.

LUNAR HIGHLANDS
The pale gray areas around the darker basins are the lunar highlands. They are covered by overlapping craters of all sizes. The asteroid impacts that formed the craters melted, broke down and remixed the various rocks that formed the Moon's original crust. Most highland rocks are complex mixtures, called breccias.

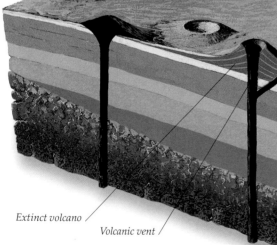

Highland region

Mare region

Sinuous rille

Straight rille

Rayed crater

Impact crater chain

Extinct volcano

Volcanic vent

Mantle rocks

Layers of crustal rocks

Old crater flooded by lava

SURFACE FEATURES
This illustration of the lunar landscape shows the border between ancient, mountainous highlands and a volcanic mare area. Lava welling up from the mantle below the crust formed the small volcanic cones. The straight rille is a valley that was created when a section of the surface sank. It split one crater in two, showing that the rille formed after the crater.

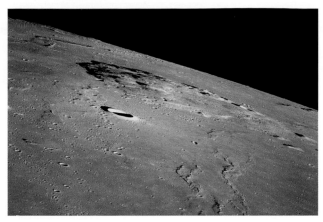

VOLCANIC DOMES
This mountain, Mons Rümker, on the Oceanus Procellarum, is a cluster of about 30 volcanic domes some 44 miles (70 km) across. They were formed by the eruption of lava through vents in the surface. Lines of cliffs called scarps, where solidifying lava piled up, are just visible on the far side of the dome (top left).

LUNAR REGOLITH
Over billions of years, meteoroids have smashed the Moon's surface rocks into a gray dust called the lunar regolith. A layer several metres deep blankets the whole Moon. It is sometimes called lunar "soil" but, unlike Earth soil, it contains no organic material. Large impacts on the Moon are now rare, but there is still a constant rain of high-speed micrometeoroids grinding down any exposed rocks. Even so, this astronaut footprint will survive millions of years in an environment with no wind or rain.

MOUNTAIN RANGES
There are 18 mountain ranges on the Moon. Most form the rims of huge impact basins and all have official Latin names. This range, the Montes Agricola, was named after the 16th-century German scientist Georgius Agricola. It stretches for 87 miles (140 km) on the eastern edge of the Oceanus Procellarum. The highest lunar mountains rise to over 15,750 ft (4,800 m).

Terraced crater rim

Central peak of crater

Ancient lava flow

SINUOUS RILLES
A valley on the Moon is called a rille or a rima. Some rilles meander across the lunar surface looking like dried-up riverbeds. In fact, they are channels created by flows of molten lava and often begin near an extinct volcano. This system of rilles is on the Oceanus Procellarum, near an ancient flooded crater (top).

Geological hammer

Feather

SHARP SHADOWS
Because the Moon has no atmosphere to scatter sunlight, its sky is always black—unlike on Earth, where the atmosphere scatters the sunlight and makes its sky look blue. During the day, the ground is brightly lit by the intense Sun. Shadows are sharp and very dark. Without a blanket of air to hold warmth, the temperature swings dramatically between day and night. The Moon is also eerily silent because there is no air to carry sound.

GRAVITY ON THE MOON
The Moon's surface gravity is only one-sixth of Earth's. To demonstrate one of the effects of this low gravity, the Apollo 14 astronaut Alan Shepard hit a golf ball nearly half a mile (0.8 km) on the Moon. The reduced gravity, together with the lack of air resistance, meant the ball went much farther than on Earth. On the next Apollo mission, Dave Scott dropped a geological hammer and a falcon feather at the same time to show they would land together though one was heavier than the other. This experiment would be impossible on Earth, where air resistance would slow down the feather more than the hammer because of the feather's shape.

Craters

Asteroid Itokawa

CRATERS ARE PITS IN the ground surrounded by raised walls. Astronomers once thought that all lunar craters were volcanic. Then in 1965, a spacecraft returned images of impact craters on Mars. Now, more scientists took seriously the theory that craters are often formed by impacting comets, asteroids, and meteoroids. The Apollo missions proved that almost all lunar craters were created by impacts. Moon craters range from microscopic pits to vast basins, such as the South Pole–Aitken Basin, which is 1,615 miles (2,600 km) across and one of the largest in the solar system.

VOLCANIC CRATERS
Volcanoes can create two different types of craters. The first are cinder cones, with pitlike craters at their summit, where ash and lava spew out and pile up over several eruptions. These cinder cone craters are on Santiago Island, in the Galapagos Islands. The second are calderas, which form when a large volume of magma is ejected in a huge volcanic eruption and the ground subsides into the emptied space.

Impactor strikes lunar surface

Impactor strikes

Ejected material

Surface compressed by shock

Explosion on impact

Impactor vaporizes

Surface rocks melt

Crater formation

Steep sides collapse

Crater shape after collapse

Crater walls slump

Terraced wall

Humpy central peak

IMPACT CRATERS
Small impactors (meteoroids) make simple, bowl-shaped craters. Larger ones (the largest are called asteroids) make craters with a more complex shape. These diagrams show an asteroid 6 miles (10 km) across traveling at tens of miles a second making a crater up to 120 miles (200 km) across.

CRATER PEAKS
When powerful impacts caused by asteroids and meteoroids excavate large craters, rock rebounds toward the center of the crater and forms a humpy cluster of peaks. The steep rim walls collapse so they look like a series of terraces. This is a crater on the Moon's far side. It is called Daedalus, and measures 58 miles (93 km) across.

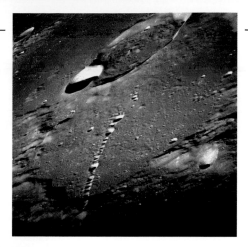

DAVY CRATER CHAIN
This chain of craters stretches for 29 miles (47 km) across the floor of the crater called Davy Y. It probably formed when the pieces of a meteoroid that had broken up crashed down one after another. There are 23 craters, each ½–2 miles (1–3 km) across. Crater chains are not very common, but there are several on our Moon and on the moons of other planets.

METEOR CRATER
Meteor Crater in Arizona, US, was created about 49,000 years ago by an impactor weighing thousands of tons, which had probably broken up in the atmosphere. Most of the object was destroyed on impact, but about 20 tons (18 metric tons) of pieces called meteorites have been found. The crater is about 560 ft (170 m) deep and 4,000 ft (1,200 m) wide.

YOUNGER CRATERS
These small, sharp-looking craters lie on the Oceanus Procellarum. The craters on the lunar maria all formed after the maria themselves. Younger craters have had less time than older ones to be worn down by micrometeoroids. The walls, and the ejected material surrounding younger craters, are usually bright and light-colored because the freshly blasted rocks only darken over time.

RAY SYSTEMS
Bright ray systems extend for vast distances around some young craters. The rays are a mixture of material blasted out by the impactor and rocks thrown up where the ejected material landed. The Tycho Crater formed 109 million years ago—that's young in lunar history. Its rays are up to 1,250 miles (2,000 km) long and make it visible to the naked eye from Earth.

MULTIRING BASIN
The most powerful impacts formed huge multiring basins. The Mare Orientale, on the western edge of the near side, is one of the largest on the Moon. Three circular rings of mountains surround the dark mare at the center. The outermost ring is the Cordillera mountain scarp, which is almost 560 miles (900 km) across.

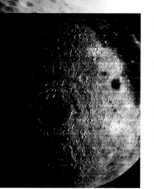

FLOODED CRATER
The Moon's oldest craters formed before volcanic activity on the Moon stopped. Lava flooded some of them, leaving only the top rims of their walls visible. This flooded crater is Thomson, which forms most of the small Mare Ingenii on the lunar far side. It is 73 miles (117 km) in diameter.

Moon rock

BASALT MOON ROCK
Basalts are dark solidified lava rocks. Lunar basalts are found in the mare areas. They are similar to rocks produced by volcanoes on Earth. This sample is full of holes, called vesicles, caused by gas bubbles in the molten lava.

COLLECTING SAMPLES
Apollo astronauts used a variety of tools to collect lunar rocks. They dragged special rakes through the regolith to sweep up small samples larger than about ½ in (1 cm). They also used scoops to collect lunar soil (regolith), hammers to break chips off large rocks, and drills and core tubes to get samples from below the lunar surface.

APOLLO ASTRONAUTS COLLECTED 842 lbs (382 kg) of rock samples. Moon rocks look similar to Earth rocks, but have a distinct composition. They were all formed when the young Moon was hot. Since the Moon has no water, there are no rocks that need water to form, such as sandstone or limestone. Unlike on Earth, the Moon's oldest rocks have not been changed by water, weather, and moving continents, so they can tell us about the earliest history of the solar system.

STUDYING SAMPLES
Lunar rocks brought back by Apollo astronauts are stored in the Lunar Sample Building at the Johnson Space Center in Houston, Texas. They are handled inside special cabinets filled with pure nitrogen so they do not get altered by contact with air.

GEOLOGY OF THE MOON
This geological map of the Moon's near side uses different colors to show which types of rock are found on the surface and how long they have been there. The large red areas are mare regions where the rock is solidified lava. The craters that formed most recently, and the ejected material around them, look like splashes of yellow. Some that are a little older are colored green. The pale blue area on the left is part of the huge impact basin that has the Mare Orientale at its centre. The oldest rocks are shown as dark brown and pink.

Lunar rover used to get to the collection site

Seismometer to measure moonquakes

*Green for
moderately young
crater Aristoteles*

*Red for
the
volcanic
rocks of
Mare
Crisium*

*Yellow for
young crater
Langrenus*

*Brown for old
rocks of southern
highlands*

FIRST ROCK FROM THE MOON
The first astronauts on the Moon collected 49 lbs (22 kg) of rock samples. Some went on display in September 1969 in Washington DC, US. There was enormous interest. Press reporters competed to get the first pictures and thousands of people lined up for hours to see the rocks for themselves.

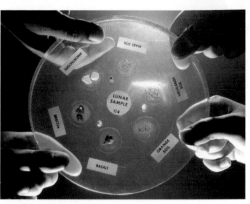

MOON ROCK CLOSE UP
You don't have to be an astronaut to get a close look at a Moon rock. Here, children are holding one of the sealed disks containing a variety of different Moon rocks, available on loan from NASA. Several museums have a Moon rock that visitors can actually touch.

LUNAR METEORITES
Over 100 meteorites found on Earth, weighing a total of 101 lbs (46 kg), are lunar rocks. Some of the material blasted out of the lunar surface by impacts in the past escaped the Moon's gravity. Some of these rocks were eventually set on a collision course with Earth. Scientists know they came from the Moon because they are similar to the Apollo samples. Many have been found in Antarctica in an area where meteorites are concentrated in the ice. Their identification is helped by the fact that dark rocks show up against the white ice.

*Apollo 17 astronaut
Harrison Schmitt*

Rock samples

*Rake for
collecting samples*

Gnomon (measuring scale)

Other moons

A TOTAL OF OVER 150 MOONS orbit the eight major planets of the solar system. Earth's moon is the fifth largest and one of only seven really large moons. Earth is the only planet with a moon so large compared with its own size. Most moons measure just a few miles across, and many belong to the huge families swarming around Jupiter and Saturn. These two giant planets each have more than 60 moons. The two innermost planets, Mercury and Venus, have no moons.

GANYMEDE
(3,270 miles/5,262 km in diameter)
Jupiter's largest moon is also the largest in the solar system.

COMPARING MOONS
No two moons in the solar system are the same. Ganymede and Titan are both slightly bigger than the planet Mercury. Large moons are globe-shaped and some have a layered interior like Earth's. Small moons generally have irregular shapes. Some moons are rocky, while many in the outer solar system are coated with a thick ice layer.

TITAN (3,200 miles/5,151 km)
Saturn's largest moon has a thick atmosphere.

Huygens probe with heat shield

Hills about 197 ft (60 m) high

CALLISTO (2,995 miles/4,820 km)
Jupiter's second largest moon is heavily cratered.

Area of 2½ sq miles (6.25 sq km)

Section of Titan's surface

TITAN EXPLORED
In January 2005, the Cassini spacecraft went into orbit around Saturn and released the Huygens probe, which parachuted down through Titan's atmosphere. This view of Titan's landscape was made from images collected during its 147-minute descent. The different colors show differences in height. Titan and the Moon are the only moons where a spacecraft has landed. Titan's surface is hidden from normal view by an orange haze in its nitrogen atmosphere, but infrared cameras and radar on board Cassini have shown that Titan has impact craters and lakes of liquid methane.

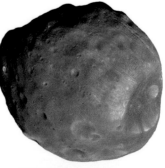

CAPTURED MOONS
The smallest moons of the solar system are almost certainly asteroids, captured by gravity when they strayed too close to the planets. Mars has two of them. Phobos, shown here, is only 17 miles (27 km) long. Deimos is even smaller with a length of 10 miles (16 km).

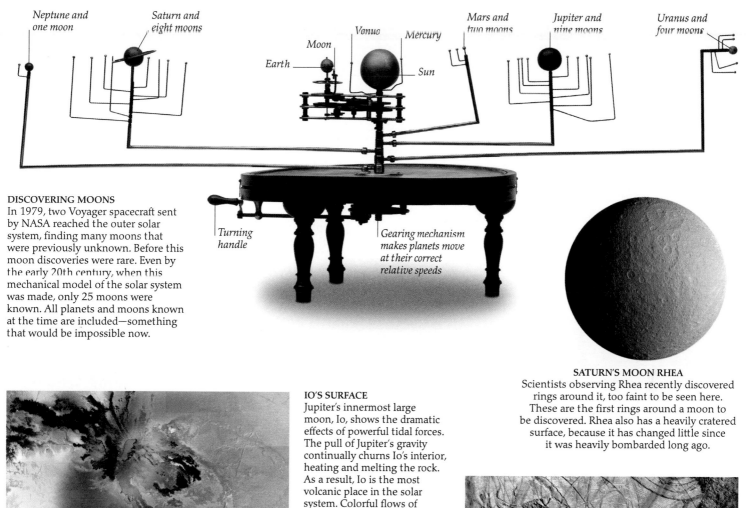

Neptune and one moon

Saturn and eight moons

Earth

Moon

Venus

Mercury

Sun

Mars and two moons

Jupiter and nine moons

Uranus and four moons

Turning handle

Gearing mechanism makes planets move at their correct relative speeds

DISCOVERING MOONS
In 1979, two Voyager spacecraft sent by NASA reached the outer solar system, finding many moons that were previously unknown. Before this moon discoveries were rare. Even by the early 20th century, when this mechanical model of the solar system was made, only 25 moons were known. All planets and moons known at the time are included—something that would be impossible now.

IO'S SURFACE
Jupiter's innermost large moon, Io, shows the dramatic effects of powerful tidal forces. The pull of Jupiter's gravity continually churns Io's interior, heating and melting the rock. As a result, Io is the most volcanic place in the solar system. Colorful flows of lava spew out onto the surface through more than 100 vents. Any impact craters that once existed have long ago been covered up. In this picture, lava is spilling out on all sides of a volcanic crater.

SATURN'S MOON RHEA
Scientists observing Rhea recently discovered rings around it, too faint to be seen here. These are the first rings around a moon to be discovered. Rhea also has a heavily cratered surface, because it has changed little since it was heavily bombarded long ago.

EUROPA'S SURFACE
Next out from Io is Europa, and its interior is also affected by Jupiter's gravity. It is covered by an icy crust several miles deep. Underneath is an ocean of liquid or slush. Europa's surface has changed greatly since it first formed and most of its impact craters have disappeared.

IO (2,263 miles/3,643 km)
The third largest of Jupiter's moons is volcanically active.

MOON (2,160 miles/3,475 km)
Earth's is the only large moon not orbiting a giant planet.

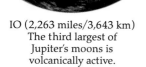

RHEA (950 miles/1,529 km)
Saturn's second largest moon is the ninth largest in the solar system.

EUROPA (1,940 miles/3,122 km)
Jupiter's fourth largest moon has sub-surface oceans.

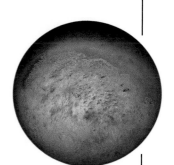

TRITON (1,682 miles/2,707 km)
Neptune's largest moon has icy plume eruptions.

One of Galileo's telescopes

The telescope era

DETAILED MAPPING OF FEATURES ON the Moon began in the early 17th century, soon after lenses and telescopes were invented. Early mapmakers made drawings while observing through a telescope, which called for great skill and patience. They invented names for lunar features and added them to their maps. Through the 18th and 19th centuries, maps of the Moon greatly improved, and the first photograph of the Moon was taken in 1839. Early ideas that the Moon was a world like Earth with water and life-forms were rejected as telescopes improved and the Moon could be seen more clearly. Even so, mistaken volcanic theories for the origin of craters persisted (see page 24). Some astronomers continued to look for changes on the Moon's surface that might be due to volcanoes.

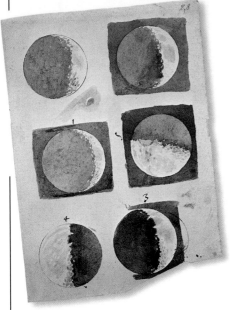

GALILEO'S SKETCHES
Italian astronomer and mathemetician Galileo Galilei was the first person to observe the Moon with a telescope in a systematic way. He began his observations in 1609, and the following year published engravings of his drawings in his book *Sidereus Nuncius* ("The Starry Messenger"). He described the Moon as being like another Earth. Galileo's drawings and a manuscript of his book are kept in Florence, where he was buried.

RUSSELL'S GLOBE
John Russell (1745–1806) was a successful English artist and portrait painter who also took an interest in astronomy. He made accurate drawings of the Moon from his own telescopic observations over 40 years. In 1797, he used them to make a globe showing the features on the Moon's near side. He also invented a special mount for the globe. Its gears reproduced the motion of the Moon, including libration, and a small globe represented Earth. Russell's Moon globe was 12 in (30 cm) across and made from papier mâché.

Van Langren named the mare we now call Mare Fecunditatis "Mare Langrenianum" after himself

A drawing from Schröter's book showing the Crater Vitello, toward the southwest of the Moon's near side

Lunar equator

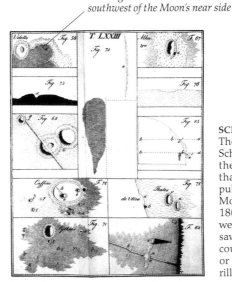

VAN LANGREN'S MOON MAP
The earliest maps of the Moon were drawn between about 1630 and 1660. The first proper map was this one, made in 1645 by a Flemish mapmaker named Michiel Van Langren (c. 1600–1675). He was the first person to call the light parts of the surface *terra* (Latin for "land") and the dark areas *mare* ("sea") or *oceanus* ("ocean"). He also introduced the idea of naming craters after famous people.

SCHRÖTER'S LUNAR DRAWINGS
The German astronomer Johann Schröter (1745–1816) drew parts of the Moon on a much larger scale than anyone had done before, and published an important book on the Moon in two volumes in 1791 and 1802. He realized that the mare areas were not water but he thought he saw changes in them, which he said could be volcanic activity, vegetation, or clouds. He discovered the lunar rille now called Schröter's Valley.

Gearing to
turn the Moon

Lunar latitude scale

Gearing to
turn Earth

Earth

Mount

IMAGINARY LANDSCAPE
This 1874 illustration depicts an eclipse of the Sun
by Earth on the Moon. It was published in *The
Moon: Considered as a Planet a World and a Satellite* by
James Nasmyth and James Carpenter, who tried to
explain craters on the Moon with a volcanic theory.

PATRICK MOORE AND TLPs
Reports of temporary changes on the Moon
(transient lunar phenomena, or TLPs) peaked
during the 1960s and 1970s. In 1969, Patrick Moore,
an enthusiastic amateur observer, worked with a
professional scientist to compile a list of 579
reported TLPs. The list later grew to over 1,000.
Many reports are due only to the changing angle of
sunlight, and are not changes in the Moon's surface.

Finder telescope

Digital
camera
attached to
back of
telescope

MONITORING FOR CHANGES
No volcanic event has ever been
confirmed on the Moon. Automatic
telescopes like this one, monitoring
the dark part of the Moon, regularly
spot flashes when meteoroids land
and record them. In May 2006, a new
crater about 46 ft (14 m) wide was
created in the Mare Nubium.

From dream to reality

FABLES AND FANTASIES ABOUT TRAVELING to the Moon have existed for centuries, but the earliest realistic stories about space travel were by the French writer Jules Verne and by other science fiction writers such as English author H. G. Wells. Verne thought of firing a spacecraft from a massive gun, and Wells came up with an imaginary antigravity material. The Russian inventor Konstantin Tsiolkovsky realized that only a rocket would work, but could not put any of his theories into practice. The American Robert Goddard had similar ideas and started to build rockets. Meanwhile, the idea of future travel to the Moon and beyond caught the public imagination and became a popular theme in films and comics.

JULES VERNE'S NOVEL
Jules Verne's story *From the Earth to the Moon*, published in 1865, was the first science fiction novel about travel to the Moon. Despite its scientific errors, it became a classic.

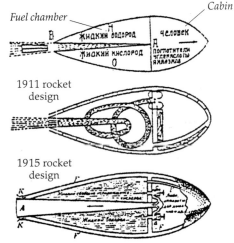

Fuel chamber

Cabin

1911 rocket design

1915 rocket design

EARLY THEORIES
Konstantin Tsiolkovsky was the first person to set out the theory of rocket propulsion. These are three of his drawings. The top one, dating from 1903, is the earliest known diagram of a liquid-fueled rocket.

ROCKET PIONEER
Robert Goddard's early interest in spaceflight was inspired by reading the novels of Jules Verne and H. G. Wells. In 1926, he launched the first ever liquid-fueled rocket. He continued to develop and test ever larger liquid-fueled rockets until 1941, when he worked for the US Navy in World War II. His pioneering work paved the way for space travel. Goddard dreamed of seeing a rocket go to the Moon, but died much before that in 1945.

Robert Goddard in 1940

Rocket lands in the Moon's eye

Rocket engine exhaust nozzle

FUNNY FACE
The first film on the theme of travel to the Moon was made in 1902 by the French director Georges Méliès. *Le Voyage dans la Lune* ("Voyage to the Moon") was a 14-minute silent movie inspired by the novels of Jules Verne and *The First Men in the Moon* by H. G. Wells. It poked fun at science and did not pretend to be realistic.

THE ROCKET AS A WEAPON
Rockets were greatly improved in the 1930s and 1940s, but for carrying warheads rather than space travel. Germany, the first country to use a rocket-propelled weapon, launched its V-2 rocket in 1942, during World War II. After the war ended in 1945, the new rocket technology was also adapted for the exploration of space. The V-2 rocket shown here is from an air show held in 1951.

A FRIEND FOR AMERICA
Wernher von Braun was in charge of Germany's wartime rocket program but, in 1945, he surrendered to the US Army and then moved to the US. He was a driving force behind the development of the rockets needed for the US space program, including the Saturn V rocket that would ultimately take astronauts to the Moon.

Experimental rocket without casing

Film poster from 1950

"DESTINATION MOON"
After World War II, writers and film directors tried to make their space stories more scientifically accurate and took advice from experts. The landmark 1950 film *Destination Moon* aimed for great realism and was a huge commercial success—its technical advisor was Herman Oberth, a Romanian aeronautics pioneer. Wernher von Braun was the technical advisor for three television films about space made by Walt Disney in the 1950s.

TINTIN ON THE MOON
Space travel to the Moon was a popular theme for stories in the 1950s. A young reporter, Tintin, was the hero of a series of comic-strip books created by Hergé, a Belgian writer and illustrator. Tintin's two Moon adventures, *Destination Moon* and *Explorers on the Moon*, were published in 1953 and 1954. This is the cover of the original French edition of *Explorers on the Moon*.

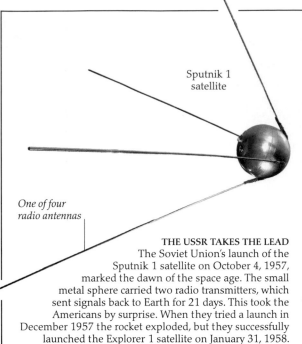

Sputnik 1
satellite

*One of four
radio antennas*

The space race

IN THE LATE 1950S, a race began between the US and the Soviet Union. Each wanted to be the first to achieve important goals in space. This space race took place at a time known as the "Cold War," when political relations between the US and the USSR (Union of Soviet Socialist Republics, or Soviet Union) were extremely tense. Initially the USSR was ahead of the US. Programs began in both countries to train astronauts and gain experience of spaceflight. From 1961 onward, landing people on the Moon became the main goal of the space race, after US President John F. Kennedy declared that America's goal was to reach the Moon by the end of the 1960s. Both sides worked on developing spacecraft that could go to the Moon and back, and on rockets powerful enough to get them there.

THE USSR TAKES THE LEAD
The Soviet Union's launch of the Sputnik 1 satellite on October 4, 1957, marked the dawn of the space age. The small metal sphere carried two radio transmitters, which sent signals back to Earth for 21 days. This took the Americans by surprise. When they tried a launch in December 1957 the rocket exploded, but they successfully launched the Explorer 1 satellite on January 31, 1958.

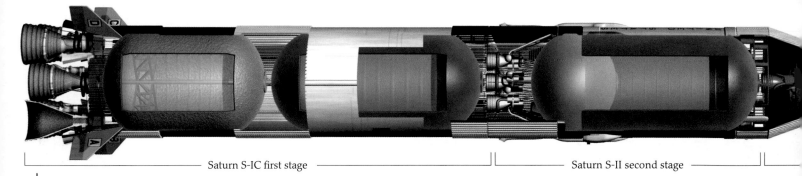

Saturn S-IC first stage — Saturn S-II second stage

THE FIRST MAN IN SPACE
On April 12, 1961, the Soviet cosmonaut Yuri Gagarin became the first person to go into space. After one orbit of Earth in Vostok 1, Gagarin operated his ejector seat and parachuted clear, during the spacecraft's descent, from a height of 4½ miles (7 km). The USSR was so secretive that it did not reveal what the outside of the spacecraft looked like until 1965.

Gagarin in the space capsule before launch

THE COLD WAR
Mistrust and rivalry between the US and the USSR began about 1917, when the USSR became a communist country after the Russian revolution. Tensions became much worse immediately after World War II, when the former Allies, which included the US and the USSR, could not agree on the future of Europe. Both countries wanted to build up their military strength and international prestige. This parade in Moscow in 1962 displayed the USSR's military might.

KENNEDY'S CHALLENGE

Six weeks after the first manned space flight by the USSR, America turned the space race into a race for the Moon. In a speech to the US Congress on May 25, 1961, President John F. Kennedy set an ambitious target for the US—to land astronauts on the Moon before 1970. At the time, America's total experience of human spaceflight was a 15-minute flight made less than three weeks earlier by Alan Shepard in the Mercury capsule Freedom 7. He had not even completed one full orbit of Earth.

THE MERCURY SEVEN

The first Americans recruited as astronauts were seven Air Force pilots, who became known as the Mercury Seven. The Mercury program's goal was to put an astronaut in orbit around Earth in a capsule holding one person. John Glenn made the first orbital flight on February 20, 1962, and three more followed. The longest was 22 orbits, made by Gordon Cooper in May 1963.

Escape rocket

Saturn S-IVB third stage — Apollo spacecraft

SATURN V ROCKET

The US developed the three-stage Saturn V rocket specially to send astronauts to the Moon. It was the largest and most powerful rocket ever launched. Including the escape rocket on top, it stood nearly 364 ft (111 m) high and weighed over 2,975 tons (2,700 metric tons). The first and second stages each had five engines and fell away in turn when their fuel ran out. The third stage, with one engine, did not separate until it had sent the Apollo spacecraft out of Earth orbit and on course for the Moon.

GEMINI 7 CAPSULE

After the Mercury missions, America's Gemini program was the next step to prepare for the Apollo Moon landings. The Gemini capsules carried two pilots. The goal of the Gemini program was to perfect space techniques, such as docking spacecraft together and space walks. These flights also gave astronauts the experience they needed to undertake a mission to the Moon. There were 10 manned Gemini flights between March 1965 and November 1966. Gemini 7 was the longest, lasting 14 days.

Outer insulation

Reentry module

SANDWICHES FOR SPACE

Gemini 3 astronaut John Young got into trouble for smuggling a corned beef sandwich on board, which his companion Gus Grissom ate. Young had disobeyed orders and the loose crumbs could have been dangerous inside the spacecraft. Here, Apollo 12 Commander Charles Conrad has a sandwich put in a pocket on his spacesuit, but there is no record that this one made it into space!

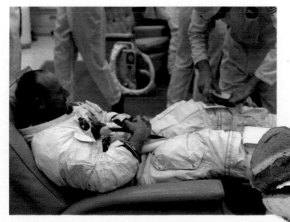

A corned beef sandwich

THE FIRST SPACEWALK

Soviet cosmonaut Aleksei Leonov made the first spacewalk on March 18, 1965, two months before the first spacewalk by an American. Leonov was on board Voskhod 2, the first two-person space mission. This is a 1960s Russian postcard of Leonov.

Destination Moon

One of the first images
of the Moon's far side,
taken by Luna 3

IN THE 10 YEARS BEFORE humans reached the Moon, the
US launched 21 unmanned lunar spacecraft while the USSR
launched 18. These missions were designed to test technologies,
make maps of the Moon, and find out whether its surface was
solid enough to land on. Many did not succeed, especially in the
early days. In the race for the Moon, the USSR crossed some
important hurdles first—the first man-made object on the Moon,
the first pictures of the lunar far side, the first soft landing on the
Moon, and the first lunar satellite. But the US was not far
behind, and by 1967 its Lunar Orbiters were scouting
for sites where the first astronauts would land.

LUNA 2

The first spacecraft sent to the Moon
were simple hard landers, intended to crash
into the surface. Soft landers could touch
down gently without damage and continue
working. Luna 1 was launched by the USSR
in January 1959, but it missed the Moon
by 3,747 miles (5,995 km). In September
1959, the Soviets tried again to hit the
Moon with Luna 2. It crash-landed
close to the crater Aristarchus.
Luna 2 was the first man-made
object to travel from Earth and
land on another body in space.

*Gas jet
to control
orientation*

*Radio
communication
antenna*

*Spacecraft
is (47 in)
120 cm long*

*Metal
sphere
47 in
(120 cm)
across*

*Sensor for
magnetic
field*

*Instruments and
transmitters in
metal cylinder*

*250 ft (76 m)
radio dish*

TRACKING LUNA 2

The Soviet Union was very secretive
about its early Moon missions, so
British astronomers at the Jodrell Bank
Observatory near Manchester were
surprised when the Soviets told them
how to track the signals from Luna 2
with their giant radio telescope. The
Director of the Observatory, Bernard Lovell,
announced on September 13, 1959, that
the signals from Luna 2 had stopped
suddenly, which meant that it had been
successfully crashed on the Moon.

LUNA 3

In 1959, the Soviet spacecraft Luna 3 swung
around the back of the Moon and returned the
first images of the lunar far side. They were
taken from a distance of about 40,000 miles
(65,000 km). Luna 3 took 29 photographs
covering 70 percent of the Moon's far side on
October 7, but the first attempts to transmit the
pictures back to Earth did not work. However,
17 fuzzy views were picked up about 10 days
later when Luna 3 came nearer to Earth again.

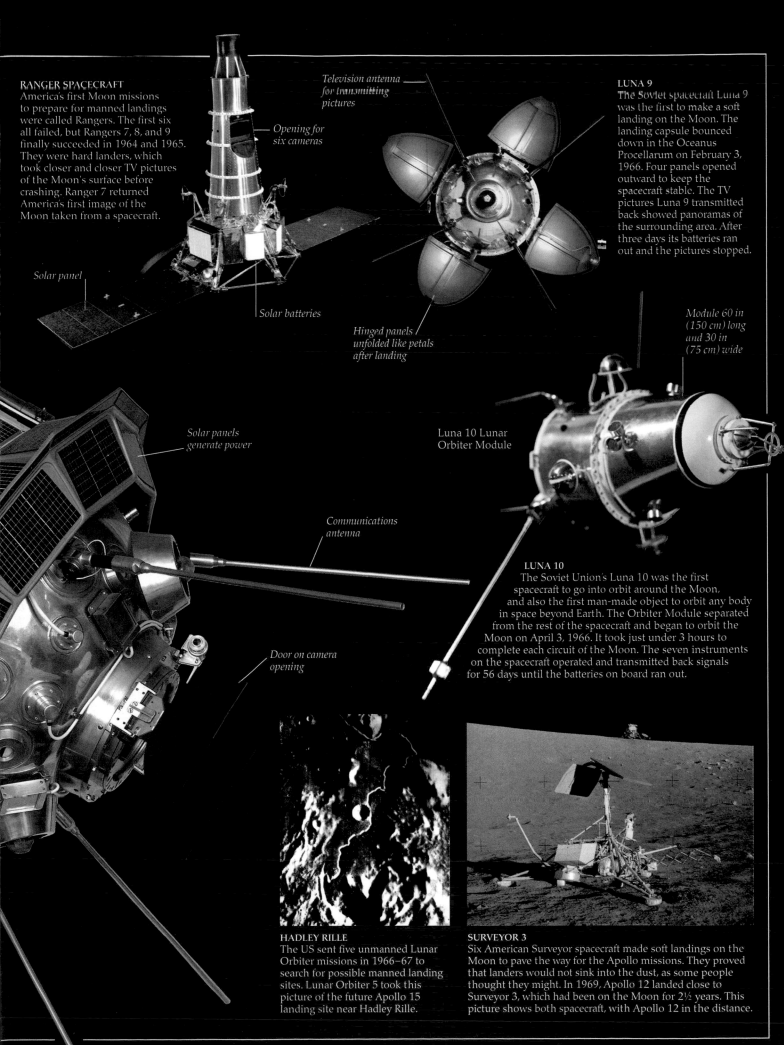

RANGER SPACECRAFT
America's first Moon missions to prepare for manned landings were called Rangers. The first six all failed, but Rangers 7, 8, and 9 finally succeeded in 1964 and 1965. They were hard landers, which took closer and closer TV pictures of the Moon's surface before crashing. Ranger 7 returned America's first image of the Moon taken from a spacecraft.

Television antenna for transmitting pictures

Opening for six cameras

Solar panel

Solar batteries

LUNA 9
The Soviet spacecraft Luna 9 was the first to make a soft landing on the Moon. The landing capsule bounced down in the Oceanus Procellarum on February 3, 1966. Four panels opened outward to keep the spacecraft stable. The TV pictures Luna 9 transmitted back showed panoramas of the surrounding area. After three days its batteries ran out and the pictures stopped.

Hinged panels unfolded like petals after landing

Module 60 in (150 cm) long and 30 in (75 cm) wide

Solar panels generate power

Luna 10 Lunar Orbiter Module

Communications antenna

LUNA 10
The Soviet Union's Luna 10 was the first spacecraft to go into orbit around the Moon, and also the first man-made object to orbit any body in space beyond Earth. The Orbiter Module separated from the rest of the spacecraft and began to orbit the Moon on April 3, 1966. It took just under 3 hours to complete each circuit of the Moon. The seven instruments on the spacecraft operated and transmitted back signals for 56 days until the batteries on board ran out.

Door on camera opening

HADLEY RILLE
The US sent five unmanned Lunar Orbiter missions in 1966–67 to search for possible manned landing sites. Lunar Orbiter 5 took this picture of the future Apollo 15 landing site near Hadley Rille.

SURVEYOR 3
Six American Surveyor spacecraft made soft landings on the Moon to pave the way for the Apollo missions. They proved that landers would not sink into the dust, as some people thought they might. In 1969, Apollo 12 landed close to Surveyor 3, which had been on the Moon for 2½ years. This picture shows both spacecraft, with Apollo 12 in the distance.

Apollo spacecraft

EACH APOLLO SPACECRAFT CONSISTED OF three parts: the Command Module (CM), the Service Module (SM), and the Lunar Module (LM). The crew of three astronauts would live in the CM on the journey from Earth and back. The SM contained fuel and equipment for supplying oxygen, water, and electricity to the CM. For most of the mission, the Command and Service Modules (CSM) were designed to remain docked together. The LM would dock with them only on the outward journey. On the spacecraft's return, the CM would separate from the SM before entering Earth's atmosphere. The CM with the astronauts inside would then splash down in the ocean.

THE THREE MODULES
The conical Command Module was about 11½ ft (3.5 m) high. The control panel inside it had 24 instrument displays, 71 lights, and 560 switches. The Service Module was a cylinder about 25 ft (7.6 m) long and 13 ft (4 m) wide. It had one main engine and small motors for performing maneuvers. The Lunar Module with its two stages stood 23 ft (7 m) tall.

Forward heat shield

Quick-escape hatch

Command Module

Instrument panel

Astronauts' seats

Service Module

Fuel tanks

Engine nozzle

Helium tanks

Fuel cells

LAUNCHING APOLLO
Apollo spacecraft were launched by Saturn V rockets from Cape Canaveral in Florida. The small escape rocket on top was designed to blast the Command Module clear if there was an emergency during the launch. The red gantry beside the rocket supported it and provided access for astronauts and technicians. After the rocket ignited, the gantry swung away. Then, with a tremendous roar and a billow of smoke, the rocket soared upward with glowing hot gas streaming behind it.

COMMAND AND SERVICE MODULES IN ORBIT
While the Mission Commander and Lunar Module Pilot went down to the Moon's surface in the Lunar Module, the Command Module Pilot stayed with the Command and Service Modules in orbit around the Moon. This picture of the Apollo 17 CSM was taken through the window of the LM.

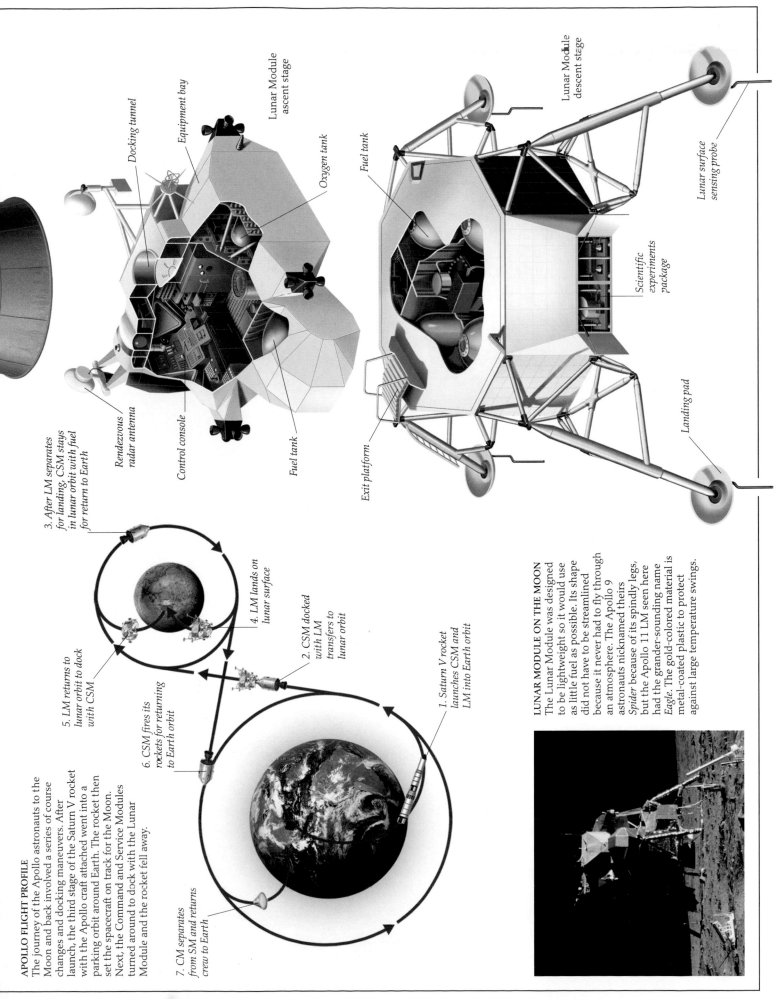

Docking tunnel

Equipment bay

Lunar Module ascent stage

Lunar Module descent stage

Oxygen tank

Fuel tank

Rendezvous radar antenna

Control console

Fuel tank

Scientific experiments package

Lunar surface sensing probe

Exit platform

Landing pad

APOLLO FLIGHT PROFILE
The journey of the Apollo astronauts to the Moon and back involved a series of course changes and docking maneuvers. After launch, the third stage of the Saturn V rocket with the Apollo craft attached went into a parking orbit around Earth. The rocket then set the spacecraft on track for the Moon. Next, the Command and Service Modules turned around to dock with the Lunar Module and the rocket fell away.

3. After LM separates for landing, CSM stays in lunar orbit with fuel for return to Earth

5. LM returns to lunar orbit to dock with CSM

4. LM lands on lunar surface

6. CSM fires its rockets for returning to Earth orbit

2. CSM docked with LM transfers to lunar orbit

1. Saturn V rocket launches CSM and LM into Earth orbit

7. CM separates from SM and returns crew to Earth

LUNAR MODULE ON THE MOON
The Lunar Module was designed to be lightweight so it would use as little fuel as possible. Its shape did not have to be streamlined because it never had to fly through an atmosphere. The Apollo 9 astronauts nicknamed theirs *Spider* because of its spindly legs, but the Apollo 11 LM seen here had the grander-sounding name *Eagle*. The gold-colored material is metal-coated plastic to protect against large temperature swings.

Getting men on the Moon

Aᴛᴇʀ sɪx ʏᴇᴀʀs ᴏғ ᴘʟᴀɴɴɪɴɢ and preparation, and a tragic fire, Apollo spaceflights began in 1968 with a series of unmanned tests (tests without a crew). All launches took place at Cape Canaveral in Florida, where the gigantic Vehicle Assembly Building was built. It was large enough to house four Saturn V rockets at a time. Apollo 7, which orbited Earth for 11 days in October 1968, was the first Apollo mission to carry a crew. Apollos 7, 8, 9, and 10 tested everything apart from the actual Moon landing.

Portable life support system

Astronaut John Young

Technician

ASTRONAUT TRAINING
The Apollo astronauts were trained for everything they might need to do on the Moon. They spent many hours in spacecraft simulators at the Manned Spacecraft Center (now called the Johnson Space Center) in Houston, Texas, and practiced in spacesuits for activities on the lunar surface. Here, Apollo 16 astronauts are learning how to use a special tool to collect lunar soil samples. John Young is reaching over a boulder to collect a sample because the soil behind it is less likely to be contaminated by dust from the astronauts' boots.

WRECKAGE OF APOLLO 1
The first Apollo spacecraft was due to lift off on February 21, 1967, but on January 27 a catastrophic fire broke out in the Command Module (CM) during a training exercise on the launch pad. The three astronauts in the Module died. This tragedy was a huge setback for the Apollo program. Afterward, the CM was redesigned with a quick-escape hatch.

HISTORIC SIGHT
Apollo 8 was the first manned spacecraft to orbit the Moon. It lifted off on December 21, 1968, and returned six days later after orbiting the Moon 10 times. The astronauts who flew on Apollo 8 were the first humans to see the entire Earth from space and to see the far side of the Moon. They took dramatic photographs, like this one, showing Earth rising over the Moon. Seeing our home planet as a whole, looking so fragile in the vast emptiness of space, made a deep impression on the astronauts and on everyone who saw their pictures.

Snoopy as NASA's space safety mascot

SNOOPY AND APOLLO 10
After the Apollo 1 disaster, NASA started a campaign to improve safety and to rebuild the devastated Apollo program. The mascot for the new program was the cartoon character Snoopy the beagle, chosen because of his refusal to accept defeat. The Apollo 10 astronauts nicknamed their Lunar Module "Snoopy" and their Command and Service Module "Charlie Brown." Charlie Brown is Snoopy's owner in the *Peanuts* cartoons.

Astronaut Charles Duke

Camera

Sampling head for soil collection tool

MISSION CONTROL
The Apollo Mission Control room was built at the Manned Spacecraft Center in Houston, Texas. As soon as the rocket left the launch pad the controllers took charge. They monitored the spacecraft and the astronauts. Controllers were in constant voice contact with the astronauts, except for a 45-minute period on each orbit when they were behind the Moon.

TRACKING SPACECRAFT
Mission controllers used radio communications to keep in contact with Apollo spacecraft and astronauts. Signals were sent and received by a network of 12 stations on the ground, one ship, and four jet aircraft. To be able to pick up faint signals from the Moon and transmit to it strongly enough at any time, three stations were spaced around the world, each with 85-ft (26-m) dishes. This one was near Canberra, Australia. The others were in Spain and California.

Mount with motor for turning the dish and tracking across the sky

Reflector mounted over dish directs radio waves into receiver

Radio waves bounce off main dish to reflector

Dressed for space

Astronauts in space and on the Moon would have to wear spacesuits to survive the absence of an atmosphere. Spacesuits were designed with many different layers underneath the outer layer and various components to protect astronauts from the dangers of space and keep them feeling comfortable. They would maintain the same pressure as Earth's atmosphere, provide the oxygen needed to breathe, and get rid of the carbon dioxide breathed out. Wearing a spacesuit, an astronaut would be protected against extremes of heat and cold, dangerous ultraviolet radiation from the Sun, and impacts of micrometeoroids.

THE APOLLO SPACESUIT
Each Apollo astronaut had three spacesuits made to fit him. In order to walk about and work on the Moon, their spacesuits had to be light and flexible. Next to their skin they wore a nylon liquid-cooled undergarment that kept them cool. Over that came the pressure garment that maintained a constant pressure, then many layers to insulate against heat and cold, and finally two layers of Teflon-coated cloth for further protection against heat. The helmet and gloves joined onto the suit with airtight seals. Overshoes went on top of the spacesuit boots for walking on the Moon.

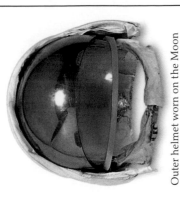

Outer helmet worn on the Moon has adjustable Sun shields and visors

Inner helmet seals to suit and maintains correct pressure inside

Communications cap includes microphone and earphones

Gold-plated visor reduces heat and glare from Sun and lunar surface

Connection to PLSS water supply

Penlight pocket

Extravehicular glove worn on lunar surface

Communications connector

Connection to emergency oxygen supply

Connection to PLSS standard oxygen supply

LOUSMA

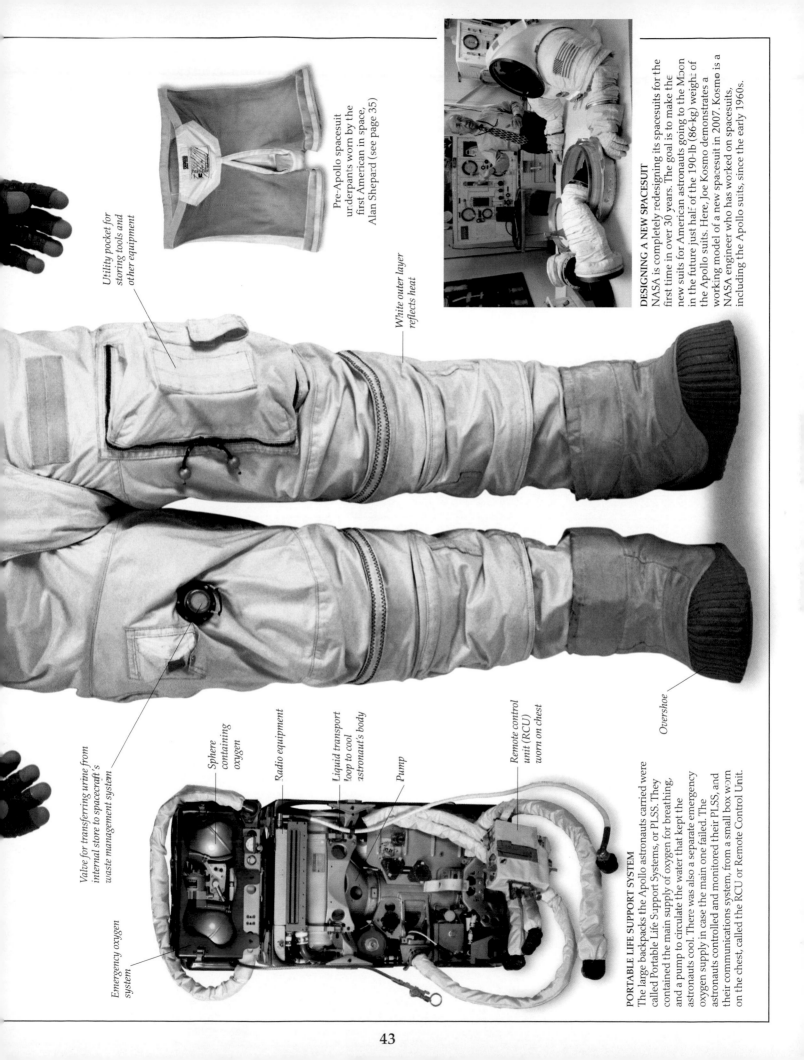

Pre-Apollo spacesuit underpants worn by the first American in space, Alan Shepard (see page 35)

Utility pocket for storing tools and other equipment

White outer layer reflects heat

DESIGNING A NEW SPACESUIT
NASA is completely redesigning its spacesuits for the first time in over 30 years. The goal is to make the new suits for American astronauts going to the Moon in the future just half of the 190-lb (86-kg) weight of the Apollo suits. Here, Joe Kosmo demonstrates a working model of a new spacesuit in 2007. Kosmo is a NASA engineer who has worked on spacesuits, including the Apollo suits, since the early 1960s.

Valve for transferring urine from internal store to spacecraft's waste management system

Emergency oxygen system

Sphere containing oxygen

Radio equipment

Liquid transport loop to cool astronaut's body

Pump

Remote control unit (RCU) worn on chest

Overshoe

PORTABLE LIFE SUPPORT SYSTEM
The large backpacks the Apollo astronauts carried were called Portable Life Support Systems, or PLSS. They contained the main supply of oxygen for breathing, and a pump to circulate the water that kept the astronauts cool. There was also a separate emergency oxygen supply in case the main one failed. The astronauts controlled and monitored their PLSS, and their communications system, from a small box worn on the chest, called the RCU or Remote Control Unit.

A giant leap

On July 21, 1969, Apollo 11 Commander Neil Armstrong made history when he stepped off the foot pad of *Eagle*, the Lunar Module, and onto the Moon's surface. Millions around the world heard him say the now famous words, "That's one small step for a man, one giant leap for mankind." Buzz Aldrin joined him on the lunar surface a few minutes later. Meanwhile, about 60 miles (100 km) above them, Michael Collins was orbiting the Moon in *Columbia*, the Command and Service Module.

LAUNCHING INTO HISTORY
Apollo 11 lifted off from Cape Canaveral (now the Kennedy Space Center) at 9:32 a.m. local time on Wednesday July 16, 1969. It was a warm sunny day and 5,000 invited guests were watching, along with 3,497 reporters and cameramen. Thousands more people crowded nearby roads and waterways jostling for a view. TV cameras on the ground followed the rocket into the sky for nearly 7 minutes after blastoff. Pictures from a TV camera mounted on the Lunar Module were later beamed live to audiences on Earth.

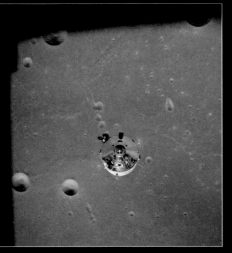

EAGLE **AND** *COLUMBIA* **SEPARATE**
A day after arriving in lunar orbit, Armstrong and Aldrin moved into *Eagle*. *Eagle* then separated from *Columbia*. The astronauts took this picture of *Columbia* through one of *Eagle*'s windows as they prepared to descend. Armstrong skillfully piloted *Eagle* to the lunar surface, avoiding large boulders. About two hours after leaving *Columbia* behind, they were safely on the ground—with just enough fuel left in the descent-stage engines for another 20 seconds of flying!

MAN ON THE MOON
About 15 minutes after Neil Armstrong stepped onto the Moon, Buzz Aldrin followed him down the ladder. The two astronauts set up an American flag, though not to claim any territory on the Moon. A TV camera mounted on *Eagle* captured pictures of Buzz Aldrin saluting the flag, while Neil Armstrong held the flagpole steady in the soft lunar soil. These were beamed around the world. Because Armstrong was the chief photographer, no photographs were taken of him on the Moon. The flag was later blown over when *Eagle* took off.

Horizontal crossbar holds flag up in the absence of any wind

LUNAR EXPERIMENTS

Armstrong and Aldrin worked together on the lunar surface for about 90 minutes. They collected 46 lb (21 kg) of rock and soil samples, took hundreds of photographs, and set up experiments to leave behind. Here Buzz Aldrin is assembling a lunar seismometer to detect moonquakes. They also set up a detector to find out about particles from the Sun, and a reflector for laser beams shot from Earth, to measure the Moon's distance precisely (see page 11).

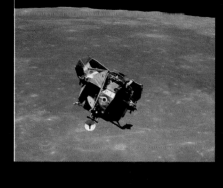

LUNAR MODULE ASCENDS

After 21 hours 36 minutes on the Moon's surface, Armstrong and Aldrin fired the ascent stage engines of *Eagle* to return to lunar orbit. They left what they no longer needed on the Moon, as well as mementos of their landing. Michael Collins took this photograph of *Eagle* as it approached *Columbia*. The two spacecraft docked so Armstrong and Aldrin could get back into *Columbia*. Then they separated again and *Eagle* was left behind.

Astronaut Buzz Aldrin

SPLASHDOWN

Columbia splashed down on July 24 in the Pacific Ocean, southwest of Hawaii. It was met by nine ships and 54 aircraft. Three swimmers from a helicopter picked up the astronauts and transferred them to an aircraft carrier, the *USS Hornet*. The astronauts wore biological isolation suits in case they had brought back microbes from the Moon.

A HEROES' WELCOME

The Apollo 11 astronauts were kept in isolation for three weeks but immediately afterward America welcomed them as heroes. New York City celebrated with a traditional ticker-tape parade on August 13. The astronauts rode in an open car along Broadway while confetti and shredded office paper rained down from the buildings on either side.

Exploring the Moon

Aᴛᴛᴇʀ Aᴘᴏʟʟᴏ 11 ᴛʜᴇʀᴇ ᴡᴇʀᴇ five more Moon landings, ending with Apollo 17 in December 1972. Apollo 13 was a near disaster and did not land on the Moon, although the crew returned safely. Each mission was more ambitious than the last. The crew of Apollo 15 had the first Lunar Roving Vehicle, improved life-support systems, and a redesigned Lunar Module. This doubled the time that could be spent on the lunar surface and increased the area the astronauts could explore.

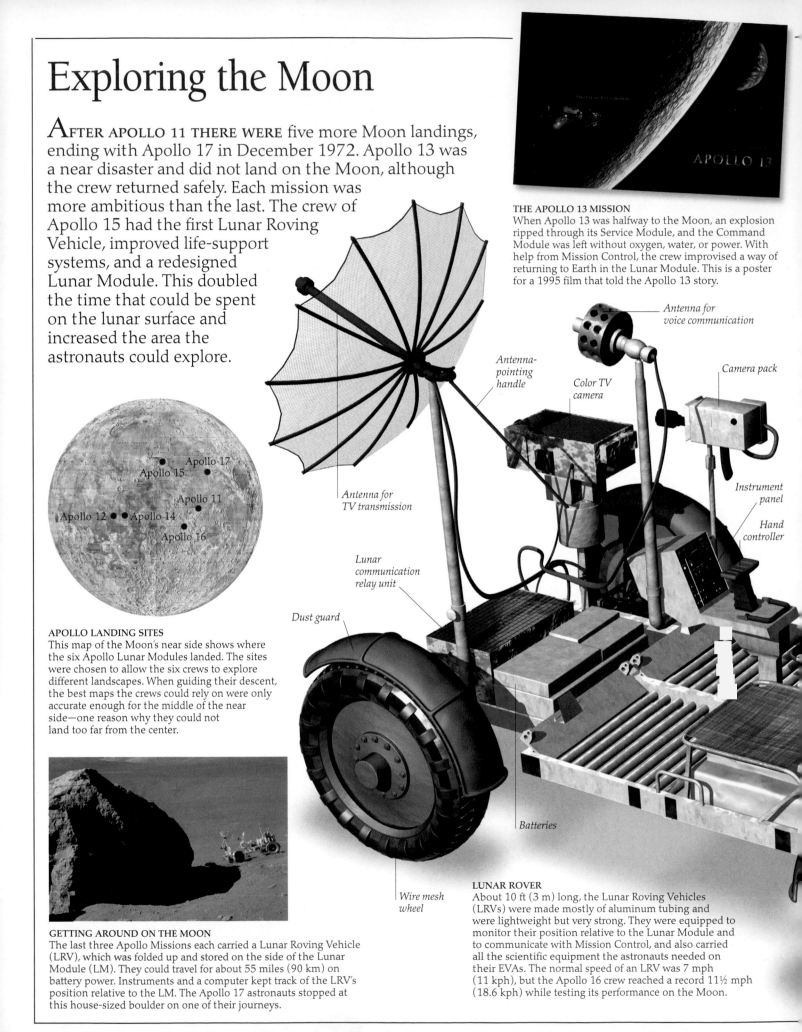

THE APOLLO 13 MISSION
When Apollo 13 was halfway to the Moon, an explosion ripped through its Service Module, and the Command Module was left without oxygen, water, or power. With help from Mission Control, the crew improvised a way of returning to Earth in the Lunar Module. This is a poster for a 1995 film that told the Apollo 13 story.

APOLLO 13

Apollo 17
Apollo 15
Apollo 11
Apollo 12 ● ● Apollo 14
Apollo 16

Antenna for TV transmission

Antenna-pointing handle

Antenna for voice communication

Color TV camera

Camera pack

Instrument panel

Hand controller

Lunar communication relay unit

Dust guard

Batteries

Wire mesh wheel

APOLLO LANDING SITES
This map of the Moon's near side shows where the six Apollo Lunar Modules landed. The sites were chosen to allow the six crews to explore different landscapes. When guiding their descent, the best maps the crews could rely on were only accurate enough for the middle of the near side—one reason why they could not land too far from the center.

GETTING AROUND ON THE MOON
The last three Apollo Missions each carried a Lunar Roving Vehicle (LRV), which was folded up and stored on the side of the Lunar Module (LM). They could travel for about 55 miles (90 km) on battery power. Instruments and a computer kept track of the LRV's position relative to the LM. The Apollo 17 astronauts stopped at this house-sized boulder on one of their journeys.

LUNAR ROVER
About 10 ft (3 m) long, the Lunar Roving Vehicles (LRVs) were made mostly of aluminum tubing and were lightweight but very strong. They were equipped to monitor their position relative to the Lunar Module and to communicate with Mission Control, and also carried all the scientific equipment the astronauts needed on their EVAs. The normal speed of an LRV was 7 mph (11 kph), but the Apollo 16 crew reached a record 11½ mph (18.6 kph) while testing its performance on the Moon.

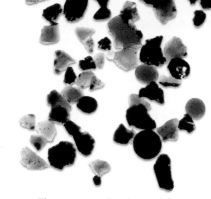

APOLLO 17 ROUTE MAP
The Apollo 17 astronauts spent nearly three days on the Moon, including 22 hours outside the Lunar Module. They made three journeys, totalling 21 miles (35 km), which are shown on this map. Each trip was called an Extra Vehicular Activity, or EVA. The pale ovals are craters and the numbers mark the places where the astronauts stopped to collect samples.

These orange glass lunar soil particles are between 0.0008 in (0.02 mm) and 0.0018 in (0.045 mm) across

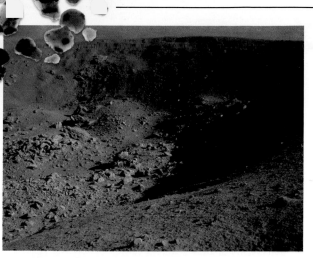

SHORTY CRATER
When the Apollo 17 astronauts visited Shorty Crater, Harrison Schmitt noticed some orange-colored soil on its rim. Though the crater had been formed by an impact, there were some cinder cones nearby—a sign of past volcanic activity. The soil contained microscopic orange glass beads, formed 3.64 billion years ago when lava shot out of a volcano like a fountain of fire.

Tongs for picking up samples

Lunar sample collection storage

Seats of tubular aluminum with nylon covers

APOLLO MISSION PATCHES
The individual patches for the Apollo missions were designed by the astronauts themselves or based on their ideas. For instance, the Apollo 11 patch included an eagle, because that was the Lunar Module's name. The Apollo 12 patch pictured a clipper ship because the Command and Service Module was named *Yankee Clipper*.

Antares *was the name of the Apollo 14 Lunar Module*

MISSION PLAQUE
All the Apollo Lunar Modules carried a commemorative plaque, which was left behind on the Moon along with the Module. They were made of stainless steel and curved to fit around one of the rungs of the ladder. Each one reproduces the signatures of the three astronauts. The signature of the US President was also on the first and last Apollo plaques. This is the plaque from the Apollo 14 mission.

Further Soviet exploration

IN THE RACE TO LAND men on the Moon, the USSR fell behind the US after Sergei Korolev—the man who had been the driving force behind the Soviet space program—died suddenly in 1966. The huge N-1 rocket, with which the USSR intended to launch a Moon mission, exploded at its first test flight in 1969. The Soviets then directed their efforts at sending robotic craft to the Moon rather than humans and began developing the technology for orbiting space stations.

SOVIET PIONEER
Sergei Korolev (1907–1966) was one of the great pioneers of spaceflight. He was responsible for Sputnik 1 and the early Soviet space achievements, but the USSR kept the identity of its "Chief Spacecraft Designer" a secret until after the Cold War (see page 34) ended.

Luna 17
Luna 13
Luna 2
Luna 21
Luna 9
Luna 24
Luna 20
Luna 16

LUNAR LANDINGS
After losing the race to put a man on the Moon, the Soviets concentrated on robotic spacecraft and continued this program until 1976. This lunar near-side map shows where seven Luna spacecraft successfully made soft landings, and where Luna 2, the first spacecraft to reach the Moon, crash-landed.

Solar panels generate power

Search radar transmitter and receiver

SOYUZ SPACECRAFT
Led by Korolev, the Soviet Union developed a spacecraft for carrying cosmonauts to the Moon. They called it Soyuz—Russian for "Union". Soyuz 1 crashed in 1967, killing cosmonaut Vladimir Komarov. In 1969, Soyuz 4 and Soyuz 5 successfully docked in Earth orbit and two cosmonauts made spacewalks to move from Soyuz 5 to Soyuz 4. Russia still uses a modern version of the Soyuz spacecraft. The design shown here was in use until 1971.

Crew seating

Window

Radar for docking

Control console

Antenna

Docking assembly

Fold-away work area

Orbital Module

Storage compartments

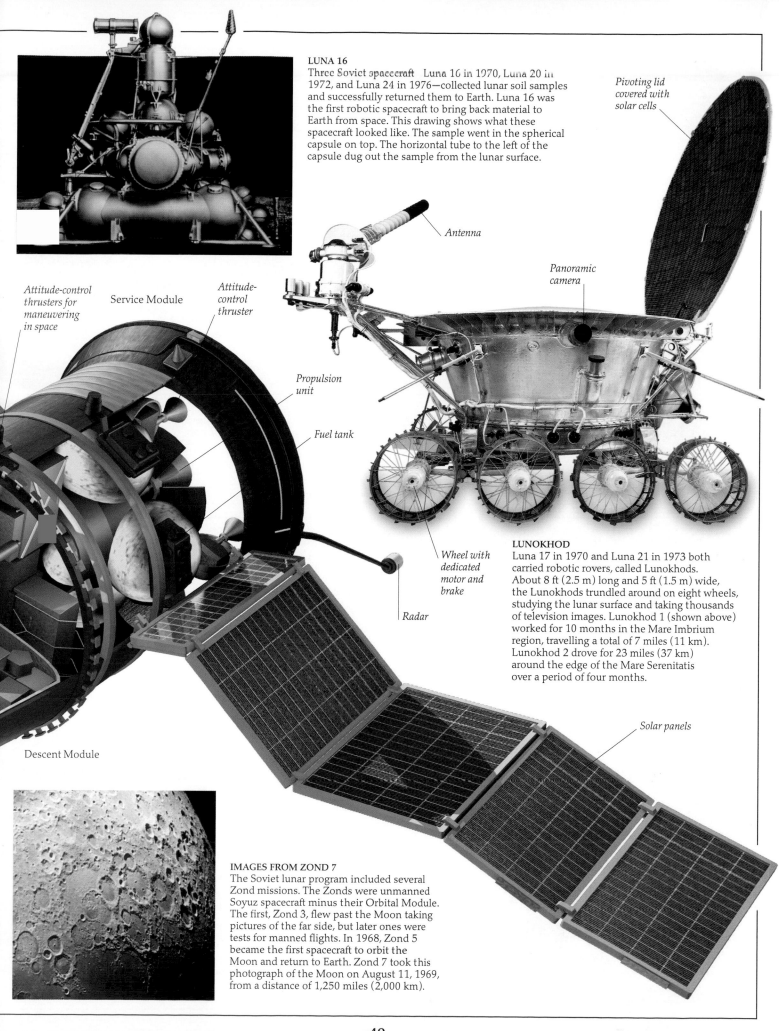

LUNA 16
Three Soviet spacecraft Luna 16 in 1970, Luna 20 in 1972, and Luna 24 in 1976—collected lunar soil samples and successfully returned them to Earth. Luna 16 was the first robotic spacecraft to bring back material to Earth from space. This drawing shows what these spacecraft looked like. The sample went in the spherical capsule on top. The horizontal tube to the left of the capsule dug out the sample from the lunar surface.

Pivoting lid covered with solar cells

Antenna

Panoramic camera

Attitude-control thrusters for maneuvering in space

Service Module

Attitude-control thruster

Propulsion unit

Fuel tank

Wheel with dedicated motor and brake

Radar

Descent Module

LUNOKHOD
Luna 17 in 1970 and Luna 21 in 1973 both carried robotic rovers, called Lunokhods. About 8 ft (2.5 m) long and 5 ft (1.5 m) wide, the Lunokhods trundled around on eight wheels, studying the lunar surface and taking thousands of television images. Lunokhod 1 (shown above) worked for 10 months in the Mare Imbrium region, travelling a total of 7 miles (11 km). Lunokhod 2 drove for 23 miles (37 km) around the edge of the Mare Serenitatis over a period of four months.

Solar panels

IMAGES FROM ZOND 7
The Soviet lunar program included several Zond missions. The Zonds were unmanned Soyuz spacecraft minus their Orbital Module. The first, Zond 3, flew past the Moon taking pictures of the far side, but later ones were tests for manned flights. In 1968, Zond 5 became the first spacecraft to orbit the Moon and return to Earth. Zond 7 took this photograph of the Moon on August 11, 1969, from a distance of 1,250 miles (2,000 km).

Living in space

SALYUT
Between 1971 and 1982, the USSR launched a series of seven space stations called Salyut (Russian for "Salute") into Earth orbit. After early failures, the last two stations were successful. Salyut 7 launched in April 1982, operated for more than 4 years, and was visited by 10 crews. This patch commemorates the Soyuz T-6's link-up with Salyut 7 in 1982.

DURING THE 1970S AND 80S, the USSR and the US focused on space stations that orbited Earth and on how their crews could live and work in space for long periods. This expertise will be vital when people explore the solar system more widely and set up bases on the Moon. The USSR launched its first space station, Salyut 1, in April 1971. The US followed with Skylab in 1973–74. America also started to develop the Space Shuttle, which first flew in 1981. Gradually, competition between the US and USSR was replaced by cooperation.

All electrical power is generated by solar panels

Solar panels are 190 ft (58 m) long

Mission badge shows Soyuz 19 and Apollo about to dock in Earth orbit

END OF THE SPACE RACE
With political relations between the US and the USSR improving in the 1970s, planning and training began for a joint space mission. A Soviet Soyuz spacecraft lifted off on July 15, 1975, with two cosmonauts on board and went into Earth orbit. A few hours later, the US launched an Apollo Command and Service Module (see page 38) with a crew of three. On July 17, the two craft connected using a specially constructed docking module, then remained together for two days. The two crews' meeting was broadcast live on TV, and they transferred between the two craft several times.

Unmanned supply craft bring supplies such as water, oxygen, fuel, food, and spare parts

EFFECTS OF MICROGRAVITY
In space, astronauts experience almost complete weightlessness—called microgravity—because they are traveling through space at the same speed as their surroundings. The bones and muscles that normally support a person's weight on the ground soon begin to waste away, and their heart and lungs do not work so well. Daily exercise helps to prevent these health problems. This picture shows astronaut Peggy Whitson exercising on a stationary cycle aboard the International Space Station.

MONTHS IN ORBIT
Salyut's successor was Mir (Russian for "Peace"). It was the first space station to be assembled in space, starting with a core module launched in 1986. Mir was occupied continuously for almost 10 years and visited by 104 people from several countries. Here Thomas Reiter plays a modified guitar on board Mir, where he spent 179 days during 1995–96 as a European Space Agency astronaut. Valery Polyakov, who was on board for 438 days, stayed the longest. After years of use, Mir was finally brought down over the south Pacific Ocean in March 2001.

THE WORLD'S SPACE STATION

Fifteen countries, led by the US, came together to construct the International Space Station (ISS), starting in 1998. The concept (shown here) was to build up the station from different modules. The final design was smaller than originally planned, with six science laboratories and accommodation for six crew members. Due for completion in 2010, the ISS is expected to be in operation for about six years.

Main truss is backbone of ISS

Port for docking spacecraft

DOCKING FOR SPACE DELIVERIES

Space stations have to be resupplied and crews transported back and forth. The Russians use Soyuz and unmanned Progress craft for this. The US is using the Space Shuttle until 2010. In a joint program that helped prepare for international cooperation on the ISS, Space Shuttles docked with the Russian space station Mir nine times between 1995 and 1998.

Solar panels turn to face the Sun

Remote sensing instruments look down on Earth

Radiators turn edge-on to the Sun to lose excess heat

Parachute helps the Shuttle slow down after landing

REUSABLE SPACECRAFT

Space Shuttles have been used for all manned NASA spaceflights since 1981. They take off attached to two rockets and an external fuel tank, and land like a glider. They have been used as orbiting laboratories, as ferries to and from space stations, for repairing and recovering satellites, and for launching satellites. Five were built for service in space. *Challenger* and *Columbia* were both destroyed in accidents and the other three, *Atlantis*, *Discovery*, and *Endeavour*, are being retired by 2010. Their final flights are helping to complete the ISS.

The new lunar invasion

BETWEEN 1961 AND 1974, THERE was at least one mission to the Moon every year, but after Luna 24 in 1976, 14 years passed before another spacecraft went to the Moon. In 1990, Japan's Hiten flew around the Moon and eventually crashed into it, but Hiten's purpose was mainly to test technology. From the 1990s, the United States' interest in exploring the Moon gradually reawakened. And now, the space agencies of Japan, China, India, and Europe are all pursuing programs to explore the Moon.

TANEGASHIMA SPACE CENTER
In January 1990, Japan became the third country after the US and the USSR to send a spacecraft to the Moon. The Japanese Space Agency launched a small spacecraft called Hiten, named after a Buddhist angel, from the Tanegashima Space Center. It entered a long elliptical orbit, which looped around Earth and the Moon. The Hiten mission was mainly a success, but contact was lost with the small, separate, lunar orbiter it released.

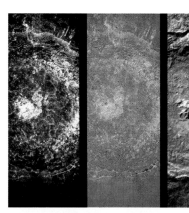

Solar panel

Octagonal spacecraft is 3¾ ft (1.14 m) across

CLEMENTINE MAPS THE MOON
The first US Moon mission after Apollo was Clementine, launched on January 25, 1994. It spent two months mapping the whole of the Moon through color filters. These pictures of the crater Tycho illustrate how this data could be used. From right to left, the images show exaggerated colors, different rock and soil types, and material relatively rich in iron and magnesium.

Clementine spacecraft

Lunar Prospector being prepared for launch

LUNAR PROSPECTOR
After Clementine, the next spacecraft the US sent to the Moon was the Lunar Prospector. This small orbiter was launched on January 7, 1998, and its mission lasted 19 months. One of the six experiments on board supported Clementine's evidence for ice in craters near the lunar poles that are always shaded from the Sun. Other scientific information gathered by the Lunar Prospector included measurements of the chemical composition of the Moon's surface.

Module to propel spacecraft into lunar orbit

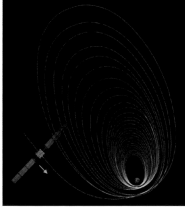

SMART-1'S SPIRAL PATH
SMART-1, launched in September 2003, was the European Space Agency's first lunar mission. It carried several miniaturized instruments but mainly tested a method of propulsion called solar powered ion drive. For 14 months, it made longer and longer elliptical orbits around Earth to reach lunar orbit, then spiraled in closer to the Moon (as shown here).

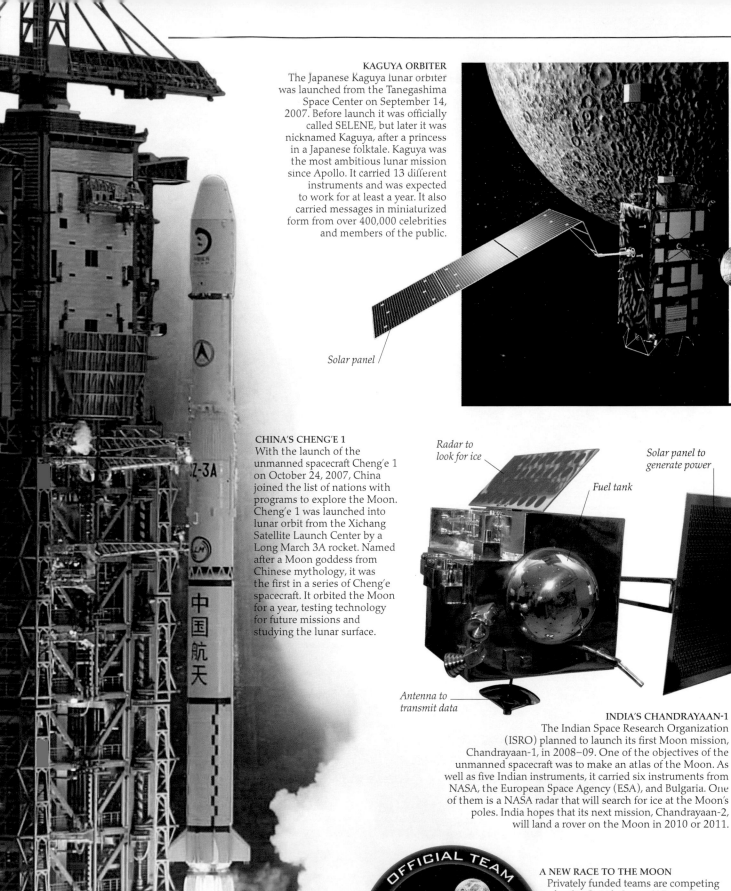

KAGUYA ORBITER
The Japanese Kaguya lunar orbiter was launched from the Tanegashima Space Center on September 14, 2007. Before launch it was officially called SELENE, but later it was nicknamed Kaguya, after a princess in a Japanese folktale. Kaguya was the most ambitious lunar mission since Apollo. It carried 13 different instruments and was expected to work for at least a year. It also carried messages in miniaturized form from over 400,000 celebrities and members of the public.

Solar panel

CHINA'S CHENG'E 1
With the launch of the unmanned spacecraft Cheng'e 1 on October 24, 2007, China joined the list of nations with programs to explore the Moon. Cheng'e 1 was launched into lunar orbit from the Xichang Satellite Launch Center by a Long March 3A rocket. Named after a Moon goddess from Chinese mythology, it was the first in a series of Cheng'e spacecraft. It orbited the Moon for a year, testing technology for future missions and studying the lunar surface.

Radar to look for ice

Solar panel to generate power

Fuel tank

Antenna to transmit data

INDIA'S CHANDRAYAAN-1
The Indian Space Research Organization (ISRO) planned to launch its first Moon mission, Chandrayaan-1, in 2008–09. One of the objectives of the unmanned spacecraft was to make an atlas of the Moon. As well as five Indian instruments, it carried six instruments from NASA, the European Space Agency (ESA), and Bulgaria. One of them is a NASA radar that will search for ice at the Moon's poles. India hopes that its next mission, Chandrayaan-2, will land a rover on the Moon in 2010 or 2011.

A NEW RACE TO THE MOON
Privately funded teams are competing for the Google Lunar X Prize. To win up to $20 million, a team has to be the first to launch, land, and operate a robot on the lunar surface by the end of 2014. The robot must travel 1,640 ft (500 m) and return images back to Earth. By 2008, 13 teams had registered.

Return to the Moon

By THE YEAR 2020, NASA plans to return humans to the Moon's surface for the first time in nearly 50 years. Its new human spaceflight program is called Project Constellation. The next generation of explorers it will send to the Moon will stay longer than their predecessors. They will travel to and from lunar orbit in a spacecraft called Orion and will descend to the Moon's surface in a lander called Altair. Two new rockets, Ares I and Ares V, will launch the astronauts in their Orion craft and everything they will need to construct a lunar base.

A NEW VISION
In January 2004, President George W. Bush proposed America's new "Vision for Space Exploration." Its goal is to send humans out to explore the solar system, beginning with a return to the Moon. Congress approved the plan and NASA began Project Constellation. The first step was to continue mapping and studying the Moon with the Lunar Reconnaissance Orbiter (LRO) in 2008–09.

THE SEARCH FOR ICE
Life on the Moon would be easier with a nearby water supply, so NASA planned to launch LCROSS (Lunar Crater Observation and Sensing Satellite) on the same rocket as the LRO. Its mission was intended to continue the search for ice on the Moon. The LCROSS shepherding spacecraft will guide part of its launch rocket to crash at high speed in an area of permanent shadow. Then it will analyze the huge plume of material thrown up for traces of water and will transmit the data back to Earth.

Control thruster

Shepherding spacecraft

Centaur upper stage rocket crashes on the Moon

The Ares I crew rocket is 309 ft (94 m) tall. It has a reusable solid rocket first stage and a liquid-fueled second stage.

ARES I AND ARES V

NASA is developing two new rockets for missions to the International Space Station and to the Moon. Ares I will take an Orion spacecraft with a crew of four to six astronauts into Earth orbit. The larger Ares V is a heavy-lift cargo launcher. It will carry hardware into Earth orbit, including a lunar lander and materials for building a lunar base. Working together, Ares I and Ares V will be able to carry 78 tons (71 metric tons) to the Moon.

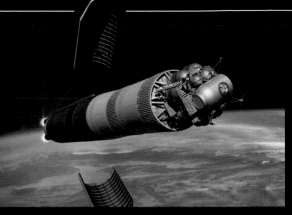

ALTAIR LANDER WITH ROCKET STAGE

An Orion crew going to the Moon will not have their lunar lander with them when they lift off. The Altair lander, combined with a rocket stage for leaving Earth orbit, will be launched separately. Orion will dock with Altair in Earth orbit, and the attached rocket stage will propel both to Moon orbit, where the crew will transfer from Orion to Altair.

ORION CREW MODULE

The Orion spacecraft will have Crew and Service Modules, similar to the Command and Service Modules of the Apollo spacecraft. At the Moon, Orion will stay in orbit while the astronauts descend to the lunar surface in the Altair lander. At the end of the mission, the astronauts will make the voyage back to Earth in the Orion Crew Module.

LUNAR OUTPOST

Orion astronauts may set up a base just outside Shackleton crater near the Moon's South Pole. Nearly continuous sunlight could provide constant power there, and frozen water may exist nearby. This radar image is colored to show the steepness of the terrain. Shackleton is at the right, with a sharp purple edge.

The Ares V cargo rocket is 358 ft (109 m) tall. It has a liquid-fueled central booster and two reusable solid rocket boosters.

LUNAR ALL TERRAIN VEHICLE

Robotic vehicles will be used to move equipment and supplies around on the Moon. They will have to be able to travel over rough ground and slopes. NASA tested this robotic vehicle, called ATHLETE, in 2008. It rolls along like a rover on its six wheels. ATHLETE's six legs can also work with feet instead of wheels, to make it a walking robot. Walking is easier than rolling for covering the most difficult terrain.

This time to stay

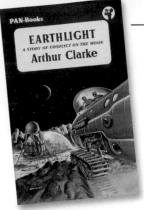

FOR DECADES, SCIENTISTS HAVE PREDICTED that there will one day be permanent stations on the Moon, and science fiction writers have dreamed about them for even longer. Several national space agencies have said they would like to set up bases on the Moon, but NASA was the first to start work on a practical plan. Starting in around 2024, it intends to build a permanent lunar base where astronauts will stay for up to six months at a time, conducting scientific studies and exploration.

A BASE ON THE MOON?
Writers and artists have long imagined what permanent human colonies on the Moon might be like. British writer Arthur C. Clarke set his 1955 story *Earthlight* 200 years after the first Moon landing. His vision is now becoming a reality.

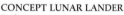

CONCEPT LUNAR LANDER
Before a permanent station is built, NASA astronauts visiting the Moon will first stay there for up to seven days in their lunar lander. NASA's planned Altair lunar lander may look similar to this, and will carry four astronauts. Like the Apollo landers, its upper section will lift off and take the crew back to the Orion Module waiting in lunar orbit for the journey home.

Steering mechanism can turn to face in any direction

Six sets of wheels can turn in any direction

Bulldozer blade can be attached here

MINING THE MOON
To operate long-term human colonies on the Moon, astronauts will have to mine some of the basic materials they need from lunar rocks and soil. This is an artist's impression of a lunar mining facility for obtaining oxygen from the volcanic soil in a mare area. Two astronauts stand next to a radio communications dish while a lunar lander takes off in the distance.

LUNAR TRANSPORTER
The astronauts who establish the first lunar base will need to move cargo around and carry out construction work on the rough terrrain. NASA has designed and tested this mobile lunar transporter for the job. Two astronauts can ride on it while standing. Each set of two wheels pivots separately so the transporter can move in any direction, including sideways. It can also be turned into a bulldozer by adding a special blade at the front.

Judge's gavel is a symbol of law and order

LUNAR LAW
From its Office for Outer Space Affairs in Vienna, the United Nations (UN) promotes cooperation between countries on the Moon and in outer space. No one owns the Moon or the land on it. Neither countries nor individuals can make territorial claims, though some businesses offer to "sell" land on the Moon.

A TENT FOR THE MOON
When astronauts first make trips to the Moon of longer than a week, they will have to take somewhere to live with them because the lander can only carry enough life support equipment for a few days. One possibility is an inflatable tent like this one, which is lightweight and easy to set up, but strong. It has heating, lighting, and an air supply inside.

FAR SIDE OBSERVATORY
The best place for most kinds of astronomical observations is beyond Earth's atmosphere, because the air distorts images and blocks much of the radiation from space aside from visible light and radio waves. The Moon is an ideal place for an observatory (above) because there is no air. Though radio observatories on Earth are not affected by the atmosphere, the far side of the Moon would be much better for them, too, because they would be protected from interference caused by man-made radio signals and electrical equipment.

Platform lowers to ground for loading and stepping on and off

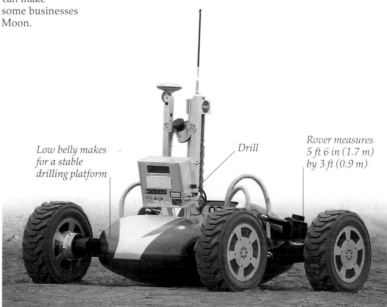

Low belly makes for a stable drilling platform

Drill

Rover measures 5 ft 6 in (1.7 m) by 3 ft (0.9 m)

DRILLING ROVER
Robotic rovers will help lunar astronauts search for the raw materials they need for life-support systems, and may even discover rare minerals that are valuable on Earth. NASA put this test rover through extreme trials at a location in the US. It uses laser sensors and a radioactive power source for working in the total darkness in shaded parts of the Moon's polar regions. The rover can raise its body to clear rocks and travel on slopes, and can drill to a depth of 3 ft 3 in (1 m).

A job on the Moon

THE FIRST ASTRONAUTS WERE ALL military pilots, but the crew of the last Apollo mission included a geologist, Harrison Schmitt, who was the first scientist to become an astronaut. Since those early days, men and women from a wide range of backgrounds in science and engineering, as well as from the armed forces, have been selected as astronauts. All are exceptional people ready to go through long and difficult training. Soon, civilians may be able to visit space as tourists more frequently. Eventually, there may be commercial flights to orbiting hotels, or even to the Moon.

Food tray to hold items down

Vacuum-packed fruits and nuts

SPACE FOODS
Astronauts in space eat three meals a day and can eat the same food as on Earth. However, all food has to be in tins or sealed packages because there are usually no refrigerators. Many foods are precooked and just need warming or water added. Salt and pepper come as liquids because floating grains could be dangerous inside the spacecraft. For the same reason, bread is banned because of the crumbs.

SELECTING ASTRONAUTS
Aspiring astronauts must first study for a degree in science or engineering. They have to be fit and healthy, with good eyesight. To go through the difficult training, they need to be brave and adventurous. They must also get along well with other people and be good at coping in difficult or dangerous situations. These newly selected astronaut candidates are experiencing near weightlessness on board a special aircraft as part of their early training.

Virgin Galactic's passenger spacecraft will be taken up 9 miles (15 km) by a mothership, then climb to 68 miles (109 km) with its own rocket.

EQUAL OPPORTUNITIES
All the Apollo astronauts were men, but today men and women compete equally to be selected as astronauts. Of nearly 500 astronauts so far, 60 have been women. This picture shows NASA astronaut Ellen Ochoa looking out of the International Space Station in 2002. She became an astronaut in 1990, flew four times on the Space Shuttle, and spent nearly 1,000 hours in space.

KEEPING FIT
In space, astronauts have to exercise every day to reduce the harmful effects of weightlessness or reduced gravity on their bones and muscles. This equipment was built for research on keeping astronauts fit. The person using it hangs horizontally while walking or running on a vertical treadmill. This closely mimics an astronaut's sensation of microgravity in orbit or on the Moon, which has just one-sixth the gravity of Earth.

TRAINING FOR THE JOB

Basic training for candidate astronauts takes two years. People who pass this can be selected to train for particular missions. Trainees learn how to carry out a variety of tasks inside and outside a spacecraft in conditions of microgravity. They practice for this under water and on special aircraft flights. Here, astronauts learn how to repair the Hubble Space Telescope using an underwater simulator.

MEETING THE PUBLIC

Only a few hundred people have so far traveled into space, and astronauts are treated as celebrities the world over. Communicating with the public is part of the job. Chinese astronauts Nie Haisheng and Fei Junlong were the crew of China's second manned space mission in 2005. After their five-day flight, they met these children in Beijing.

VIRGIN GALACTIC

Even people who are not professional astronauts may soon travel into space. From about 2009, commercial companies are planning to offer paying passengers suborbital flights, which are not as expensive and require much less preparation than going into orbit. Full orbital flights will probably be available to the public sometime in the future.

Near side

THE BEST MAPS OF THE MOON astronomers have today were made from millions of images collected by orbiting spacecraft. They are far more detailed than any maps made from observations with a telescope. The five Lunar Orbiters returned over 1,000 photographs of the whole Moon in 1966–67. Some close-ups included details only 3 ft (1 m) across. In 1994, Clementine took 1.8 million digital images. It could see down to 330 ft (100 m). Over 2,000 features on the Moon have been given names.

GOLDSTONE ANTENNA
Used as a radar dish to bounce radio signals off the Moon, this 230-ft (70-m) wide antenna in California has mapped some areas of the Moon in enough detail to show features as small as a house. It is part of NASA's Deep Space Network, which receives data from distant spacecraft and sends commands to them by radio.

COPERNICUS
The Copernicus Crater is 57 miles (91 km) across. Because of the light colored material surrounding it, and its ray system, it is an easy crater to spot from Earth. It was named after the famous Polish astronomer Nicolaus Copernicus (1473–1543). He realized that, contrary to what people believed then, Earth and the other planets orbit the Sun, and that Earth is not at the center of the solar system.

CLARISSIMUS·ET·DOCTISSIMUS·DOC
TOR·NICOLAUS·COPERNICUS·TORU
NENSIS·CANONICUS·WARMIENSIS
ASTRONOMUS·INCOMPARABILIS

RUPES RECTA
The popular name for this feature is the Straight Wall because its shadow can sometimes makes it appear like a steep cliff. However, in reality it is a gentle slope about 1½ miles (2.5 km) wide and 800–1,000 ft (240–300 m) high, caused by a fault line in the lunar surface. The fault line stretches for about 70 miles (110 km) on the eastern edge of the Mare Nubium.

fault line

MARE FRIGORIS

PLATO CRATER ►

MONS RUMKER

MONTES JURA

SINUS IRIDIUM

MONTES AGRICOLA

MARE IMBRIUM

◄ ARISTARCHUS CRATER

ERATOSTHENES CRATER ▼

MONTES

OCEANUS PROCELLARUM

MONTES CARPATUS

◄ COPERNICUS CRATER

◄ KEPLER CRATER

◄ GRIMALDI CRATER

PTOLEMAEUS CRATER ►

ALPHONSUS CRATER ►

ARZACHEL CRATER ►

◄ GASSENDI CRATER

MARE NUBIUM

RUPES RECTA

◄ BYRGIUS CRATER

MARE HUMORUM

TYCHO ► CRATER

CLAVIUS CRATER

MARE
FRIGORIS

◄ ARISTOTELES
CRATER

◄ HERCULES
CRATER

MONTES
CAUCASUS

APENNINUS

MARE
SERENITATIS

MARE
VAPORUM

PROCLUS CRATER ►

MARE
CRISIUM

MARE
TRANQUILLITATIS

MARE
FECUNDITATIS

ALBATEGNIUS
CRATER
▼

THEOPHILUS CRATER ►

CYRILLUS CRATER ►

MARE
NECTARIS

CATHARINA CRATER ►

RUPES ALTAI

HUMBOLDT ►
CRATER

PICCOLOMINI ►
CRATER

STEVINUS ►
CRATER

◄ STÖFLER
CRATER

OVERLAPPING CRATERS

This string of three large craters is easy to see with binoculars. The top one, Theophilus, is 60 miles (100 km) across and overlaps Cyrillus just below it. Beneath them is Catharina, whose circular outline has been distorted by several craters that formed later. This is a close-up of part of a color-coded map that shows the height of the lunar landscape (see below).

PLATO

Plato (c. 428–347 BCE) was a great thinker and scientist in ancient Greece. He set up the Academy in Athens, one of the first institutions of learning in the western world. He realized that the motion of the planets could be analyzed through mathematics. The crater named in his honor is 68 miles (109 km) wide. It lies just north of the Mare Imbrium and its floor is dark with flooded lava, like the nearby mare.

Plato

+8 km   +5 miles

+4   +2.5

0   0

-4   -2.5

-8   -5

HIGHLANDS AND LOWLANDS

This color-coded map shows the height of the lunar landscape above and below the average. Places at average height are shown in yellow. The pattern of the maria and the floors of large craters stands out in blue and purple, which are used for low-lying terrain. The highest places are shaded orange and red. Typically, the highland areas are 2½ miles (4 km) higher than the maria. The data was collected by the Clementine spacecraft in 1994 (see page 52).

TYCHO BRAHE

The most conspicuous crater on the Moon was named Tycho after the Danish astronomer Tycho Brahe (1546–1601), who is often known by just his first name. He died before the telescope was invented but, using instruments he built himself, he made very accurate measurements of the positions of the Sun, Moon, planets, and stars for more than 20 years. Crater Tycho, in the Moon's southern highlands, is 52 miles (85 km) in diameter.

Far side

THE SOVIET UNION CHOSE NAMES for prominent features on the Moon's far side soon after its spacecraft had taken the first photographs. These include Mare Moscoviense (Sea of Moscow) and craters named after Soviet scientists and cosmonauts. Three craters near the large Apollo crater are named after the Apollo 8 astronauts, who were the first to see the far side. New names are sometimes added, such as six approved in 2006 to honor the astronauts killed in the 2003 Space Shuttle disaster.

THE FIRST VIEW

The first images of the Moon's far side were taken by the unmanned Soviet spacecraft Luna 3 (see page 36). Although the photos were blurry, it was still a great achievement for 1959. This commemorative stamp issued by the USSR shows the spacecraft and the date when the photographs were taken.

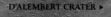

Rocket engine nozzle

Communications antenna

Communications antenna

Solar panel

Lunar Orbiter 4

Camera lenses

PHOTOGRAPHIC SURVEY

In 1966–67, the five American Lunar Orbiter spacecraft photographed 99 percent of the Moon. This was before digital photography, so the film had to be developed on board, then scanned and the pictures transmitted to Earth as radio signals. In 2007, the Lunar Orbiter Digitization Project began to convert these high-quality photographs into digital images that could be enhanced and pieced together into detailed mosaics.

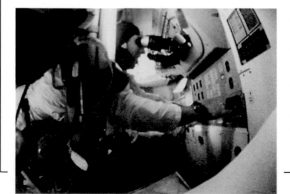

APOLLO EYEWITNESS

The only humans to have seen the Moon's far side are the astronauts who flew on Apollo missions 8 and 10 to 17. The Apollo 8 crew of Frank Borman, James Lovell, and William Anders were the first to do so when their Command Module made its first pass behind the Moon on Christmas Eve, 1968. Their first impression was of a whitish gray landscape, "like dirty beach sand," with "a lot of bumps and holes."

◀ D'ALEMBERT CRATER ▶

◀ CAMPBELL CRATER

◀ GIORDANO BRUNO CRATER

MARE MOSCOVIENSE

LACUS LUXURIAE ▶

SHAHINAZ CRATER ▶

MENDELEEV ▶ CRATER

◀ NECHO CRATER

DAEDALUS CRATER ▶

◀ GAGARIN CRATER

AITKEN ▶ CRATER

◀ TSIOLKOVSKY CRATER

VAN DE GRAAF CRATER ▼

◀ SCALIGER CRATER

MARE INGENII

JULES VERNE ▶ CRATER

LIEBNITZ CRATER ▶

PAULI CRATER ▶

VON KÁRMÁN CRATER ▶

SCHRODINGER CRATER

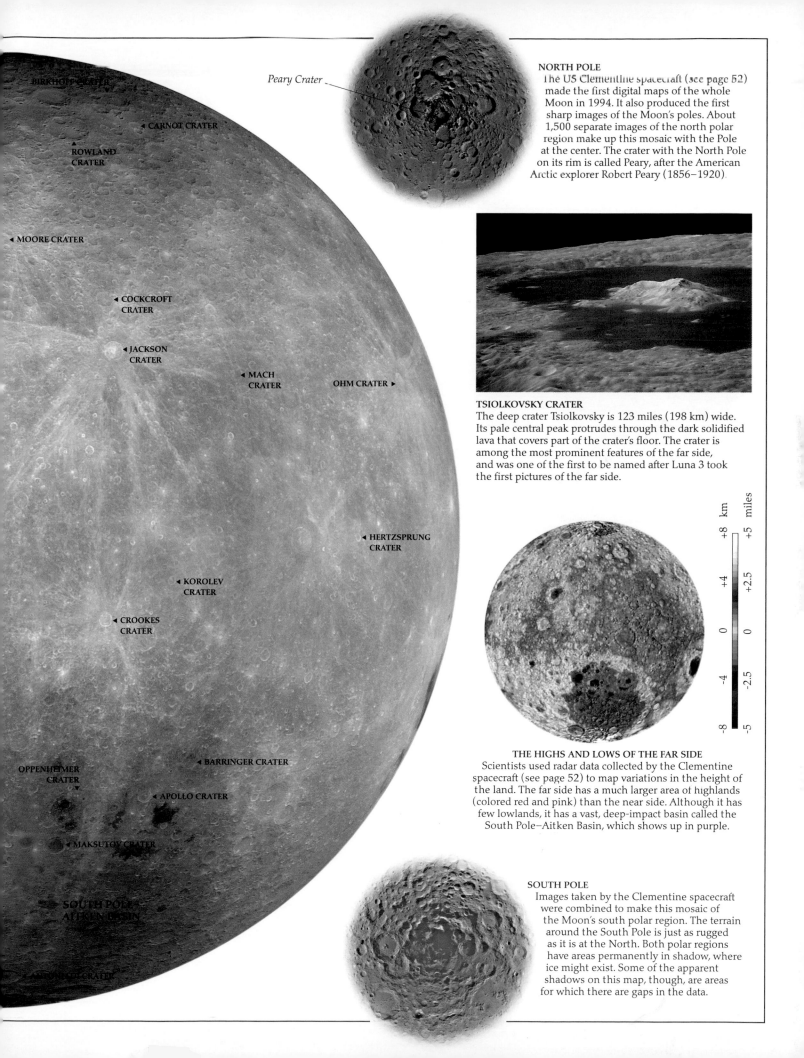

BIRKHOFF CRATER

◄ CARNOT CRATER

ROWLAND
CRATER

◄ MOORE CRATER

◄ COCKCROFT
CRATER

◄ JACKSON
CRATER

◄ MACH
CRATER

OHM CRATER ►

◄ HERTZSPRUNG
CRATER

◄ KOROLEV
CRATER

◄ CROOKES
CRATER

OPPENHEIMER
CRATER
▼

◄ BARRINGER CRATER

◄ APOLLO CRATER

◄ MAKSUTOV CRATER

SOUTH POLE–
AITKEN BASIN

Peary Crater

NORTH POLE
The US Clementine spacecraft (see page 52)
made the first digital maps of the whole
Moon in 1994. It also produced the first
sharp images of the Moon's poles. About
1,500 separate images of the north polar
region make up this mosaic with the Pole
at the center. The crater with the North Pole
on its rim is called Peary, after the American
Arctic explorer Robert Peary (1856–1920).

TSIOLKOVSKY CRATER
The deep crater Tsiolkovsky is 123 miles (198 km) wide.
Its pale central peak protrudes through the dark solidified
lava that covers part of the crater's floor. The crater is
among the most prominent features of the far side,
and was one of the first to be named after Luna 3 took
the first pictures of the far side.

km   miles
+8   +5
+4   +2.5
0   0
-4   -2.5
-8   -5

THE HIGHS AND LOWS OF THE FAR SIDE
Scientists used radar data collected by the Clementine
spacecraft (see page 52) to map variations in the height of
the land. The far side has a much larger area of highlands
(colored red and pink) than the near side. Although it has
few lowlands, it has a vast, deep-impact basin called the
South Pole–Aitken Basin, which shows up in purple.

SOUTH POLE
Images taken by the Clementine spacecraft
were combined to make this mosaic of
the Moon's south polar region. The terrain
around the South Pole is just as rugged
as it is at the North. Both polar regions
have areas permanently in shadow, where
ice might exist. Some of the apparent
shadows on this map, though, are areas
for which there are gaps in the data.

Lunar timeline

Even before there were telescopes, early astronomers followed the Moon's motion and tried to measure its distance and size. But telescopes revolutionized the mapping and scientific study of the Moon. Then, in the mid-20th century, unmanned spacecraft and the Apollo missions opened up a new way of exploring the Moon. This timeline tracks significant events in the study, understanding, and exploration of the Moon, from the first telescopic observations, through the history of lunar spacecraft and landings, to the present.

Time magazine cover from 1968

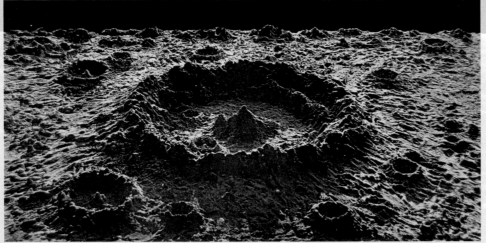

Model of a crater on the Moon, pictured in Nasmyth and Carpenter's 1874 book

JULY 26, 1609
Thomas Harriot, a British mathematician, makes the first observation of the Moon through a telescope, though he publishes no drawings until 1611.

1610
Italian astronomer Galileo Galilei publishes drawings of the Moon, which he made with the help of a telescope in late 1609.

1647
German astronomer Johannes Hevelius publishes the first reasonably accurate chart of the Moon.

1651
Italian astronomer Giovanni Riccioli establishes the system for naming craters after famous astronomers and scientists. Over 130 craters are still called by the names he gave.

1661
The first globe of the Moon is completed by the British architect and astronomer Sir Christopher Wren, who presents it to King Charles II.

1752
German astronomer Tobias Mayor publishes accurate tables of the Moon's position in the sky. They are good enough to be used by sailors for calculating their position at sea.

1834–37
German astronomers Johann Mädler and Wilhelm Beer produce the first precise map and description of the Moon. They claim that the Moon has neither an atmosphere nor water.

1839
John William Draper, a professor of chemistry in New York, takes the first photograph of the Moon.

1874
British engineer James Nasmyth and British astronomer James Carpenter publish their book, *The Moon: Considered as a Planet a World and a Satellite*. It suggests that craters on the Moon are the result of volcanic activity.

1893
American scientist Grove Karl Gilbert (1843–1918) writes correctly that lunar craters are the result of impacts, but his work is ignored.

OCTOBER 4, 1957
The USSR launches Sputnik 1, the first artificial satellite to orbit Earth, and the "space race" with the United States begins.

Laika, the first living creature in space in 1957

NOVEMBER 3, 1957
The dog Laika becomes the first living creature in space when launched aboard the USSR's Sputnik 2.

1958
The National Aeronautics and Space Administration (NASA) is founded in the US and announces Project Mercury, to launch an astronaut into space.

JANUARY 2, 1959
Luna 1, the first spacecraft to fly past the Moon, is launched by the USSR. The nearest it gets to the Moon is 3,747 miles (5,995 km) on January 4.

SEPTEMBER 12, 1959
The USSR launches Luna 2, the first human-made object to reach the Moon. It crash-lands near the crater Aristarchus on September 14.

OCTOBER 4, 1959
Luna 3 is launched by the Soviet Union. It returns the first, hazy images of the Moon's far side.

APRIL 12, 1960
The Soviet cosmonaut Yuri Gagarin becomes the first man in space when he makes a 108-minute flight around Earth in Vostok 1.

MAY 5, 1961
Alan Shepard makes a 15-minute suborbital flight in Freedom 7 and becomes the first American in space.

MAY 25, 1961
In a speech to the US Congress, President John F. Kennedy announces that an American will land on the Moon and be returned safely to Earth before the end of the decade.

JULY 28, 1964
The US launches Ranger 7, which successfully returns the first close-up images of the Moon on July 31 before crashing onto the surface as planned.

JULY 18, 1965
The USSR launches Zond 3. It takes the first clear images of the Moon's far side on July 20.

JANUARY 31, 1966
The USSR launches Luna 9. On February 1, it makes the first soft landing by a spacecraft on the Moon.

MARCH 16, 1966
NASA launches Gemini 8, which later achieves the first docking between two orbiting spacecraft.

MARCH 31, 1966
Luna 10 is launched by the USSR. It becomes the first spacecraft to go into lunar orbit.

AUGUST 10, 1966
Lunar Orbiter 1, the first US lunar orbiter, is launched by NASA. It takes photographs of the Moon in search of landing sites.

JANUARY 27, 1967
The Apollo 1 crew of Roger Chaffee, Virgil Grissom, and Edward White are killed in a fire in the Command Module (CM) during a training exercise. It takes 18 months to modify the design of the CM.

SEPTEMBER 15, 1968
The USSR launches Zond 5, which carries living material, including turtles. It is the first spacecraft to travel around the Moon and safely return to Earth, splashing down in the Indian Ocean on September 21, 1968.

OCTOBER 11, 1968
NASA launches Apollo 7, the first manned Apollo spacecraft, on an 11-day mission in Earth orbit. The crew of Walter Schirra, Donn Eisle, and R. Walter Cunningham make the first live TV transmission from space.

DECEMBER 21, 1968
Apollo 8, the first manned flight around the Moon, is launched by NASA. The crew of Frank Borman, Jim Lovell, and Bill Anders become the first people to see Earthrise over the Moon. They return on December 27.

MARCH 3–13, 1969
Apollo 9 tests in Earth orbit the spacecraft to be used for manned Moon missions. The crew for the 10-day mission consists of James McDivitt, David Scott, and Russell Schweikart.

MAY 18–26, 1969
The Apollo 10 crew of Thomas Stafford, John Young, and Eugene Cernan perform a full dress rehearsal for a Moon landing. They stop short of a touchdown.

JULY 16–24, 1969
Apollo 11 becomes the first space mission to land humans on the Moon. Neil Armstrong and Buzz Aldrin step onto the Moon on July 20, while Michael Collins remains on board the orbiting Command Module.

Buzz Aldrin steps down on the Moon on July 20, 1969

NOVEMBER 14–24, 1969
Apollo 12 lands astronauts Charles Conrad and Alan Bean on the Moon, with Richard Gordon as Command Module Pilot.

APRIL 11–17, 1970
Apollo 13 has to be aborted following an explosion on board, but the crew of James Lovell, John Swigert, and Fred Haise return to Earth safely.

SEPTEMBER 12–24, 1970
The Soviet Luna 16 becomes the first robotic spacecraft to land on the Moon and return a sample to Earth.

NOVEMBER 10, 1970–SEPTEMBER 14, 1971
The USSR's Luna 17 completes its mission. It carries Lunokhod 1, the first robotic rover to explore the Moon.

JANUARY 31–FEBRUARY 9, 1971
Apollo 14 successfully completes its Moon mission. Alan Shepard and Edgar Mitchell land while Stuart Roosa is Command Module Pilot.

JULY 26–AUGUST 7, 1971
Apollo 15 astronauts David Scott and James Irwin become the first to drive a lunar rover on the Moon. Alfred Worden is Command Module Pilot.

FEBRUARY 14, 1972
The USSR launches Luna 20. It returns with 1 oz (30 g) of lunar soil nine days later.

Japan's Hiten spacecraft, launched in 1990

APRIL 16–27, 1972
Apollo 16 astronauts John Young and Charles Duke spend 71 hours on the lunar surface, while Thomas Mattingley pilots the Command Module.

DECEMBER 7–19, 1972
In the last Apollo mission, Apollo 17, Eugene Cernan and Harrison Schmitt spend 75 hours on the Moon. Ronald Evans pilots the Command Module.

JANUARY 8–JUNE 3, 1973
The USSR's Luna 21 completes its mission, carrying the second Lunokhod robotic rover.

AUGUST 9, 1976
The USSR launches Luna 24. It returns to Earth on August 22 with 6 oz (170 g) of lunar soil.

JANUARY 24, 1990
Japan launches Hiten, and becomes the third nation (after the US and the USSR) to achieve a lunar flyby, orbit, and crash-landing.

ESA's SMART-1, launched in 2003

JANUARY 25, 1994
NASA launches Clementine into lunar orbit. It finds evidence of ice at the Moon's poles.

JANUARY 7, 1998
NASA launches Lunar Prospector carrying six scientific instruments into lunar orbit.

SEPTEMBER 27, 2003
The European Space Agency launches SMART-1, the first European spacecraft to orbit the Moon.

JANUARY 14, 2004
President Bush commits the US to a long-term human and robotic program to explore the solar system, starting with a return to the Moon.

SEPTEMBER 14, 2007
Japan launches its lunar orbiter Kaguya.

OCTOBER 24, 2007
China launches its first lunar orbiter, Chang'e 1.

2009
India plans to launch its first lunar orbiter, Chandrayaan-1.

2009
NASA hopes to launch the Lunar Reconnaissance Orbiter.

Hall of fame

MANY ASTRONOMERS HAVE MADE NOTABLE contributions to our knowledge and understanding of the Moon, from the Greeks more than 2,000 years ago to the planetary scientists of today. The Apollo Moon landings were among the most significant events for human history as well as for lunar science. The skill and courage of all the astronauts involved in the Apollo program contributed to 12 men being able to walk on the Moon.

Italian astronomer Galileo

ALDRIN, BUZZ (1930–)
Aldrin was an American astronaut who was the Apollo 11 Lunar Module pilot, and the second person to walk on the Moon. He also flew on Gemini 12 in 1966.

ANDERS, WILLIAM (1933–)
This American astronaut was one of the first three humans to orbit the Moon on Apollo 8.

ARISTARCHUS OF SAMOS (c. 310–230 BCE)
The Greek astronomer Aristarchus was the first person to try to measure the Moon's size. His method was correct, but as he could not make the required observations accurately enough, his estimate was double the correct size.

Neil Armstrong, the first man on the Moon

ARMSTRONG, NEIL (1930–)
This US astronaut, as commander of Apollo 11, became the first person to set foot on the Moon. Previously an aeronautical engineer and test pilot, Armstrong also flew with David Scott on Gemini 8, which made the first docking in space.

BEAN, ALAN (1932–)
Bean was an American astronaut who was the Apollo 12 Lunar Module pilot and one of the 12 men who landed on the Moon. In 1973 he flew on Skylab for 59 days.

BEER, WILHELM (1777–1850)
Beer was a wealthy German banker who built a private observatory. He formed a partnership with the astronomer Johann Mädler to produce the first exact map of the Moon in 1834–36, and a description of the Moon in 1837.

BLAGG, MARY (1858–1944)
Blagg was a British astronomer who worked for many years on compiling a list of features on the Moon and devising a uniform system for naming them. She was co-author of *Named Lunar Formations*, published in 1935, which became the standard reference book on the subject.

BORMAN, FRANK (1928–)
Borman was an American astronaut who, as Apollo 8 Commander, led the first crew to orbit the Moon. He was also the Commander on Gemini 7.

BROWN, ERNEST (1866–1938)
A British mathematician, Brown spent all his life studying the Moon's complicated motion. He compiled extremely accurate tables for figuring out the Moon's position, and they remained the best available until 1984, when computers began doing it more accurately.

CERNAN, EUGENE (1934–)
This American astronaut was the Commander of Apollo 17 and the last person to leave the Moon. He had previously flown on Gemini 9 and Apollo 10. He is one of only three people to have flown to the Moon twice.

CONRAD, CHARLES "PETE" (1930–1999)
This American astronaut was the Apollo 12 Commander and the third man to walk on the Moon. He also flew on Gemini 5, Gemini 11, and Skylab 2.

DUKE, CHARLES (1935–)
One of the 12 men to have landed on the Moon, this American astronaut piloted the Apollo 16 Lunar Module."

GAGARIN, YURI (1934–1968)
The first person to fly in space, Gagarin had been a fighter pilot before he was selected as a cosmonaut. He died in an air crash while training to return to space on Soyuz 3.

GALILEI, GALILEO (1564–1642)
The Italian astronomer and physicist Galileo was one of the greatest scientists of his time. He made the first astronomical telescopes, and was the first person to make detailed scientific observations of the Moon with a telescope.

GRIMALDI, FRANCESCO (1618–1663)
Grimaldi was a professor of mathematics and physics at Bologna in Italy. Though most famous for his discoveries about light, he also made accurate measurements of features on the Moon and used them to draw an important lunar map for a book on astronomy by his fellow scientist, Giovanni Riccioli.

HARTMANN, WILLIAM K. (1939–)
Hartmann is a planetary scientist who was one of the first researchers to develop the idea, now generally accepted, that the Moon formed in a giant collision. He is also well known as a leading space artist.

HEVELIUS, JOHANNES (1611–1687)
The German astronomer Hevelius published the first-ever lunar atlas in 1647. He was the son of a wealthy brewer and worked in Danzig (now Gdansk in Poland), using telescopes he designed and built himself.

Johannes Hevelius published the first-ever lunar atlas

HIPPARCHUS (c. 190–120 BCE)
Hipparchus was a Greek mathematician and astronomer, born in what is today part of Turkey. He figured out an early theory for the motion of the Moon and also accurately calculated the distance of the Moon, relative to the size of the Earth, by making observations at eclipses.

IRWIN, JAMES (1930–1991)
An American astronaut who was the Apollo 15 Lunar Module pilot, Irwin was one of the 12 astronauts to have walked on the Moon.

KOROLEV, SERGEI (1907–1966)
This Soviet rocket scientist directed the Soviet Union's Moon program until his death in 1966.

KUIPER, GERARD (1905–1973)
A Dutch–American planetary scientist, Kuiper revived interest in the scientific study of the Moon in the 1960s. He founded the Lunar and Planetary Laboratory in Arizona, US, and helped to identify possible Apollo landing sites.

LOVELL, JAMES (1928–)
This American astronaut flew around the Moon twice, on Apollo 8 and Apollo 13.

James Nasmyth cowrote an influential book about the Moon's features

MÄDLER, JOHANN HEINRICH (1794–1874)
Mädler was a German astronomer who worked in partnership with Wilhelm Beer to produce the first exact map of the Moon in 1834–36 and a description of the Moon in 1837. He invented the use of letters to identify small craters around a larger named one.

MITCHELL, EDGAR (1930–)
Edgar was an American astronaut who was the Apollo 14 Lunar Module pilot, and one of the 12 men to have walked on the Moon.

MOORE, SIR PATRICK (1923–)
The British amateur astronomer Patrick Moore is well known as a television host and author of over 100 books. His main astronomical interest has been studying and charting the Moon.

NASMYTH, JAMES (1808–1890)
Nasmyth was a successful British engineer and industrialist who took up telescope-making. He became very interested in observing the

English scientist Isaac Newton

Moon and discovering the origin of craters. He wrote an influential book, with the help of James Carpenter, a professional astronomer, and argued that lunar craters were volcanic.

NEWTON, ISAAC (1643–1727)
Newton was one of the greatest scientists of all time. He was made a professor at Cambridge University in England when only 26. His first research on gravity, in 1665, concerned the motion of the Moon. He later set out his law of universal gravitation.

RICCIOLI, GIOVANNI (1598–1671)
In 1651, this Italian astronomer published a map of the Moon, which had been drawn by Francisco Grimaldi. On this map, Riccioli gave many craters names that are still in use today.

SCHMIDT, JOHANN (1825–1884)
Schmidt was a German astronomer who spent a lifetime making drawings of the Moon from which he produced a map in 1874. It was the first map to improve on the one made by Beer and Mädler in 1834–36.

SCHMITT, HARRISON (1935–)
An American astronaut who was the Apollo 17 Lunar Module pilot, Schmitt was one of the 12 men to have walked on the Moon. Trained as a geologist, he was the first scientist-astronaut. He later served as a US Senator.

SCHRÖTER, JOHANN (1745–1816)
The German astronomer Schröter trained in law and then began a legal and administrative career. He also set up a private observatory. There he made an important study of the Moon and published books on the subject in 1791 and 1802.

SCOTT, DAVID (1932–)
Scott was an American astronaut who made three space flights. The first two were on Gemini 8 and Apollo 9. As Commander of Apollo 15, he became one of the 12 astronauts who walked on the Moon.

SHEPARD, ALAN (1923–1998)
Shepard was an astronaut who became the first American to travel into space. He was also Apollo 14 Commander and one of the 12 astronauts who landed on the Moon.

SHOEMAKER, EUGENE (1928–1997)
This American geologist founded the science of lunar and planetary geology, and showed that craters are formed by impacts. He was unable to become an astronaut because of a health problem, but the spacecraft Lunar Prospector carried some of his ashes to the Moon. The crater where it crashed was named in his honor.

VAN LANGREN, MICHIEL FLORANT (1600–1675)
The Dutch cartographer Van Langren was the first person to make a proper map of the Moon and name its features in a systematic way, though his names are no longer used.

VON BRAUN, WERNHER (1912–1977)
This German-born rocket scientist was behind the V-2 rocket of World War II but later directed the development of the Saturn rockets used for NASA's Apollo Moon program (see pages 32–33).

WEBB, JAMES (1906–1992)
Webb was the NASA Administrator in 1961–68. He used his political and administrative skills to achieve the goal set by President Kennedy of landing men on the Moon. The replacement for the Hubble Space Telescope is being named the James Webb Space Telescope in his honor.

WHITAKER, EWEN (1922–)
Whitaker is a British-born American scientist who is the leading expert on the naming of lunar features. He has written a history of lunar mapping and was responsible for a system of giving letter designations to smaller craters on the lunar far side.

YOUNG, JOHN (1930–)
This American astronaut became the first astronaut to make six flights. These were on Gemini 3, Gemini 10, Apollo 10, Apollo 16, and the first and ninth flights of the Space Shuttle. As Apollo 16 Commander he landed on the Moon, and is one of only three people to have flown to the Moon twice.

Eugene Shoemaker, the founder of lunar and planetary geology

Find out more

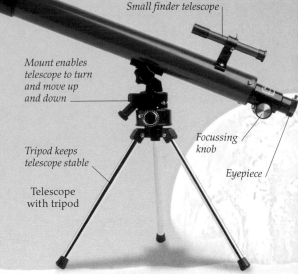

Small finder telescope

Mount enables
telescope to turn
and move up
and down

Tripod keeps
telescope stable

Telescope
with tripod

Focussing
knob

Eyepiece

THE BEST WAY TO START finding out more about the
Moon is to look at it for yourself. Even if you do not have
a telescope or binoculars, you can still make out its main
dark areas and the bright crater Tycho, which are marked
on the map on page 9. You can follow the Moon's monthly
cycle by drawing sketches or taking notes of its phases and
the dates and times when you see them. See if you can
also spot the Moon during daylight or when it is just a
thin crescent in the western sky soon after sunset.

SKETCHING THE MOON
You do not need to be good at
art to try sketching part of the
Moon. Look at some craters
near the dividing line between
the bright and dark parts of
the Moon through
binoculars or a
telescope. Their long
shadows make them
stand out. Draw simple
outlines, then shade
in the shadows.

TELESCOPES
The Moon is the easiest object in the sky to
observe with a small telescope. You will be able
to see many more features than by eye alone.
Use the map on pages 60–61 to help you
identify some of the main craters and maria.
Keep in mind that the image you see through
an astronomical telescope is usually upside
down—with south at the top.

Hold binoculars as steady
as you can or rest them
against something firm

OBSERVING THE MOON
Using binoculars is an ideal way to start exploring
the Moon in more detail. They do not have to be
special—the ordinary kind you might use for
bird-watching will do. You will get to know the
Moon best if you keep looking on different
nights when the Moon is at different phases.

Sleeping bag keeps you
warm and comfortable
when observing outside

USEFUL WEBSITES

- Lunar Picture of the Day (LPOD)
  features a different image every day:
  http://lpod.wikispaces.com/

- Find pictures and information about
  the Apollo missions here:
  http://www.apolloarchive.com/

- This site has a timeline with links to
  the details of every lunar space mission:
  **http://nssdc.gsfc.nasa.gov/planetary/
  lunar/lunartimeline.html**

- Visit NASA's eclipse site to discover
  more about past and future eclipses,
  and for a table of the Moon's phases:
  **http://eclipse.gsfc.nasa.gov/eclipse.
  html**

- Google Moon has a collection of
  interactive maps. There are also picture
  stories for each Apollo landing:
  http://www.google.com/moon/

- This page from *Sky & Telescope*
  magazine's website has helpful articles
  about observing the Moon:
  **http://www.skyandtelescope.com/
  observing/objects/moon/**

- Two NASA websites carry the latest
  news on NASA's progress toward
  returning astronauts to the Moon:
  **http://www.nasa.gov/mission_
  pages/exploration/main/index.html
  http://www.nasa.gov/mission_
  pages/constellation/main/index.html**

- For a list of all features on the Moon, visit
  http://planetarynames.wr.usgs.gov/

SPACE CENTER HOUSTON
The visitor center at NASA's Lyndon B. Johnson Space Center in Texas is called Space Center Houston. The Astronaut Gallery displays the world's best collection of spacesuits, and on the walls are photographs of every American astronaut who has flown in space. Visitors can also see real spacecraft in the Starship Gallery and take a behind-the-scenes tram tour to see parts of the Johnson Space Center.

KENNEDY SPACE CENTER
In the Apollo/Saturn V Center at the Kennedy Space Center visitor complex in Florida, visitors see this real Saturn V rocket, like the ones used to launch the Apollo astronauts to the Moon. This display is just one of many exhibits and attractions on the huge site. Visitors who are lucky might even see a rocket lift off in the distance from one of the launch pads.

Schoolchildren getting a close-up view of the spacesuit

Shenzhou 6 mission patch

Places to visit

AMERICAN MUSEUM OF NATURAL HISTORY, NEW YORK, NEW YORK
The museum's Rose Center for Earth and Space features such exhibits as:
- a gallery of more than 75 rarely seen photos from the Apollo Moon missions
- a world-class planetarium featuring a virtual field trip to the Moon and other shows

JET PROPULSION LABORATORY, PASADENA, CALIFORNIA
JPL sent the first robotic craft to the Moon in the 1960s, and today is engaged in a wide variety of space missions. Guided tours must be reserved in advance:

US SPACE AND ROCKET CENTER, HUNTSVILLE, ALABAMA
Home to the famous Space Camp program, the USSRC features:
- rides that mimic the experience of space flight
- original and replica spacecraft, including the Saturn V used in the Apollo program

SMITHSONIAN NATIONAL AIR AND SPACE MUSEUM, WASHINGTON DC, AND CHANTILLY, VIRGINIA
This museum has more spacecraft than any other in the world. The large exhibits at Chantilly, Virginia, include the Space Shuttle *Enterprise*. Among the huge number of items on show in Washington DC are:
- the actual Apollo 11 Command Module
- a piece of Moon rock visitors can touch

KENNEDY SPACE CENTER, FLORIDA
The NASA center from where all of the US's manned space flights have been launched has impressive facilities for visitors. You can:
- see a full-size Space Shuttle replica
- enter a full-size mockup of an International Space Station module
- have lunch with an astronaut

SPACE CENTER HOUSTON, TEXAS
This huge complex has a fantastic range of exhibits, demonstrations, and theaters including:
- Real Mercury, Gemini, and Apollo space capsules
  - A module that simulates living in space

CHINA AEROSPACE EXHIBITION
Keep a look out for temporary space exhibitions coming to your area. This model spacesuit was on display at a temporary Aerospace Exhibition in Chengdu, Sichuan Province, China, when the picture was taken in October 2005. The spacesuit was a special attraction because the crew of China's second manned spaceflight had successfully landed less than two weeks earlier, in their Shenzhou 6 spacecraft, after a flight of 75 Earth orbits taking nearly 5 days. They had worn suits similar to this one during the mission.

Glossary

ANTENNA
A device, usually a dish or a rod, used for receiving and/or sending radio signals.

APOGEE
The point farthest from Earth in the orbit of the Moon or of an artificial Earth satellite.

ASTEROID
A small body made of rock and/or metal orbiting the Sun.

ASTRONAUT
A person who travels into space or who has trained to do so.

ATMOSPHERE
A layer of gas surrounding a planet, moon, or star.

Cosmonaut Alexandr Kaleri

ATTITUDE CONTROL
Changing or holding a spacecraft's direction of travel.

BASALT
A dark gray rock formed when lava solidifies. It is found in the mare areas of the Moon.

BASIN
A very large impact crater, more than 190 miles (300 km) wide.

CALDERA
A large volcanic crater, formed when the top of a volcano collapses.

CHEMICAL ELEMENT
One of the basic materials of which all matter in the universe is made. About 90 occur naturally, such as oxygen, carbon, and iron.

CINDER CONE
A steep-sided cone-shaped hill around a volcanic vent where lava has erupted.

CORONA
The outer layers of the Sun, which are seen as a white halo during a total solar eclipse.

COSMONAUT
A person who travels into space under the Russian space program (or did so under the former Soviet Union's space program).

CRATER
A bowl-shaped depression in the ground, with a raised rim. Craters can be caused by an impact or by a volcano.

CRUST
The outer layers of rock on a planet or moon.

Eclipse of the Sun by the Moon

DWARF PLANET
A small planet, such as Pluto, which is spherical rather than irregular in shape and orbits the Sun as part of a belt of other small rocky or icy bodies.

ECLIPSE
When the Moon covers all or part of the Sun in the sky (solar eclipse), or when Earth's shadow is cast on the Moon (lunar eclipse).

ELLIPSE
A shape like an elongated circle.

ESCAPE VELOCITY
The speed an object needs to escape from the gravity of another body. The escape velocity from Earth's surface is about 7 miles per second (11.2 km per second).

GEOLOGIST
A scientist who studies what rocks are made of, how they formed, and how they have changed over time.

GIBBOUS
From a Latin word meaning "hump." The Moon's phase when more than half is illuminated but it is not full.

GRAVITY
Gravity is the force of attraction between two objects caused by their mass. It decreases the farther apart the objects are.

IMPACTOR
An object that hits something else, especially at high speed.

ION DRIVE
A way of propelling a spacecraft with a stream of particles made electrically.

LANDER
A spacecraft that lands on the surface of a moon or planet.

LASER
A device that produces a thin, very powerful beam of light of a specific color. Lasers can be used to determine the exact distance between the Moon and Earth.

LAUNCH VEHICLE
A rocket-powered system to lift a spacecraft into space. Often called a "rocket."

Meteorite

LAVA
Molten (liquid) rock that spews out onto the surface of a planet or moon during a volcanic eruption.

LIBRATION
The slight alteration in the part of the Moon's surface visible from Earth.

MAGMA
Underground molten rock.

MANTLE
The layer of rock inside a moon or planet that lies underneath the crust and over the core.

MARE (PLURAL MARIA)
A dark, low-lying plain on the Moon, made of solidified lava. The word comes from the Latin for "sea."

METEORITE
A piece of rock and/or metal from space that has landed on the surface of Earth, the Moon, or any other planetary body.

METEOROID
A small piece of rock in space, which is not as large as an asteroid and less than about 300 ft (100 m) across.

Launch vehicle

MICROGRAVITY
The condition of weightlessness experienced by astronauts when in orbit or in free-fall. Objects have weight on Earth and the Moon as the ground exerts an upward force the same as the downward force of gravity. Orbiting and falling objects are not beyond the pull of gravity, but they experience microgravity because they are free to accelerate toward the source of gravity.

MICROMETEOROID
A microscopic particle of dust in space.

MONTES
The Latin word for "mountains," used in the official names of mountain ranges on the Moon.

NASA
The National Aeronautics and Space Administration, the American government agency responsible for non-military activities in space.

NEBULA
A large cloud of gas and dust among the stars. The solar system, including Earth and the Moon, formed in a nebula surrounding the Sun.

OCCULTATION
When one astronomical body passes in front of and obscures another one.

OPTICAL TELESCOPE
A telescope for observing visible light.

ORBIT
The path of one astronomical body around another, or to travel along an orbit.

ORBITER
A spacecraft that goes into orbit around Earth, or a moon or planet beyond Earth.

PERIGEE
The point closest to Earth in the orbit of the Moon or of an artificial Earth satellite.

Eagle Nebula

PHASE
The proportion of the disk of the Moon (or any other astronomical object), as seen from Earth, that is illuminated with sunlight.

PLANET
One of the larger bodies orbiting the Sun, or a similar body orbiting any star. There are eight major planets in our solar system.

PLANETESIMAL
A small clump of rock and/or ice that came together when our solar system was forming. Planetesimals were up to 6 miles (10 km) across and later merged to form larger asteroids and planets.

PRESSURE
The force exerted by something over 1 sq ft (or 1 m) of area. Atmospheric pressure is the pressure due to an atmosphere, such as Earth's. Because there is no air pressure in space, spacesuits must exert pressure on astronauts' bodies or they would die.

PROBE
A package of scientific instruments released from a spacecraft or satellite to collect data about a moon or planet by traveling down through its atmospheric layers and landing on it or crashing into it.

PROMINENCE
A huge flamelike stream of gas, visible during a solar eclipse, rising off the Sun's surface.

RADAR
A method for measuring the distance of something, or mapping the shape of its surface, by bouncing radio waves off it. The word "radar" stands for RAdio Detection And Ranging.

RADIO TELESCOPE
Equipment for collecting and analyzing natural radio signals from objects in space. Most radio telescopes use a large dish to collect and focus the signals.

REGOLITH
The loose material like dust, sand, or soil found on the surface of the Moon.

RILLE
A valley on the Moon. Some were formed when surface rocks dropped down between two long cracks or faults. Others were made by lava flows. The word comes from the German for "groove."

ROCKET
An engine that makes a launch vehicle move forward by burning chemical fuel and driving hot gas backward through a nozzle. "Rocket" is also often used to mean an entire launch vehicle, including the equipment to guide and control it.

ROVER
A robotic explorer placed on the surface of a moon or planet, which can drive around on wheels, or a vehicle used by astronauts to travel on the surface of the Moon.

RUPES
A feature on the Moon that is in the shape of a cliff or a slope. From the Latin for "cliff."

SATELLITE
A small object, either natural or man-made, in orbit around a larger one.

SEISMOMETER
An instrument for collecting data about earthquakes or moonquakes.

SINUS
The Latin word for "bay," used in the names of some features on the Moon.

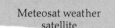
Meteosat weather satellite

SOLAR SYSTEM
The Sun and everything in orbit around it.

SPACE
Anywhere farther from Earth than about 60–75 miles (100–120 km).

SPACECRAFT
A vehicle that travels through space. Spacecraft may transport astronauts or cargo, or carry instruments to study objects in the solar system. Unmanned spacecraft in orbit around Earth are usually called satellites.

SPACEWALK
Activity by an astronaut in space outside his or her spacecraft. Spacewalks are formally called "extra-vehicular activities," or EVAs.

SPACE AGE
The present period of history in which space has been explored by humans and robots. It started in 1957 with the launch of the first artificial satellite, Sputnik 1.

SPACE RACE
The competition between the USSR and the US in the 1960s to achieve important goals in space, especially landing humans on the Moon.

SPACE STATION
A large, habitable Earth satellite, where different crews of astronauts or cosmonauts can live and conduct scientific research over periods ranging from a few days to many months.

TRANSIENT LUNAR PHENOMENON (TLP)
A temporary change on the Moon's surface.

ULTRAVIOLET RADIATION
A type of radiation similar to light, but invisible and more powerful.

VOLCANO
A place where molten rock from underground comes to the surface through a crack or tube, called a vent.

Spacewalk from the Space Shuttle

Index

Acknowledgments

Dorling Kindersley would like to thank:
Stewart J. Wild for proofreading; Hilary Bird for the index; David Ekholm JAlbum, Jenny Finch, Sunita Gahir, Susan St. Louis, & Lisa Stock for the clip art; and Sue Nicholson & Edward Kinsey for the wall chart; Margaret Parrish and John Searcy for Americanization.

The publisher would like to thank the following for their kind permission to reproduce their photographs:

(Key: a-above; b-below/bottom; c-center; l-left; r-right; t-top)
akg-images: 7cr; Bibliothèque Nationale, Paris 2cr, 66br; Bildarchiv Steffens 6tr; Alamy Images: Arco Images GmbH 23br (Feather); Flancer 12r; John Henshall 69c; Scott Hortop 13br; The London Art Archive 60clb, 67tc; mediacolor's 25tl; North Wind Picture Archives 61br; Photos 12 2tr, 32bl; David White 27tr; WorldFoto 21t; The Bridgeman Art Library: Private Collection / Bonhams, London / 56tl; Ben Bussey: 3c, 25cr, 26-27ca, 27cr, 61tc; Corbis: Yann Arthus-Bertrand 24tr; Pallava Bagla 53cr; Bettmann 19br, 45br, 64bc; Richard Cummins 69tl; EPA / Sanjeev Gupta 15bl; Hulton-Deutsch Collection 33tl; Karen Kasmauski 52tl; Yevgeny Khaldei 34bl; Roger Ressmeyer 4cra, 15ca, 15tr, 26ca, 26tl, 67br; Reuters 15br; Rykoff Collection 35br; Sean Sexton Collection 31tr, 64cl; after The Discovery of a World in the Moone, 1638 by John Wilkins 8br;

DK Images: Courtesy of The British Library, London. Shelfmark Ör.7964 p.1620 / Laurence Pordes 15tl; The British Museum, London / Peter Hayman 6tl; CONACULTA-INAH-MEX. Authorized reproduction by the Instituto Nacional de Antropología e Historia / Peter Wilson 7cl; Courtesy of Bob Gathany / Andy Crawford 42tr; NASA 50br, 70tc; National Maritime Museum, London / Tina Chambers 2b, 29t; Courtesy of The Natural History Museum, London / Colin Keates 23bl (Hammer), 70tr; Rough Guides / Tim Draper 6-7b; Rough Guides / Mark Thomas 61cra; Courtesy of The Science Museum, London / Dave King 4t, 30-31t; Courtesy of The Science Museum, London / James Stevenson 43cr; ESA: 2002 52br; 28cl, 65cr; FLPA: B. Borrell Casals 16tr, 17cra; after From the Earth to the Moon, 1865 by Jules Verne 32tl; Galaxy Picture Library: Pete Lawrence 11tr; Thierry Legault 20br; Damian Peach 60bc; Robin Scagell 10bl, 11c, 13bl; Michael Stecker 15c; Getty Images: AFP / Tim Sloan 54cl; The Bridgeman Art Library 66tr; China Photos 7tl, 69bl; Chinafotopress 57cla; Keystone 31cr; National Geographic / Otis Imboden 44tl; Time Life Pictures / NASA 26-27b; Time Life Pictures / Time Magazine 64tr; Courtesy of the X PRIZE Foundation: 53bc; Honeysuckle Creek Tracking Station (www.honeysucklecreek.net); Colin Mackellar 63tl; Imagine China: 53l; iStockphoto.com: 14t; Adrian Beesley 36bl; Courtesy of JAXA: 24tl, 65tr; Akihiro Ikeshita

53tr; The Kobal Collection: George Pal Prods 21br; Universal 46tr; Moulinsart 2008: © Hergé 33br; NASA: 8tr, 9tc, 31br, 35tl, 40tl, 43bl, 50bl, 55br, 55crb, 56bl, 56cl, 57br, 57cra, 58br, 61crb, 63cr; Ames Research Center 4bl, 52bl, 54bl; Dryden Flight Research Center 51br, 66cl; ESA / JPL / University of Arizona / USGS 28bl; ESA and The Hubble Heritage Team (STScI/AURA) 71clb; GSFC / Image created by Reto Stöckli, Nazmi El Saleous and Marit Jentoft-Nilsen 9r; Johnson Space Center 35c, 51tr, 55tr, 57tr, 58c, 71br; Johnson Space Center / Pat Rawlings (SAIC) 57tl; JPL 28cr, 28tl, 29clb, 37tl, 46cl, 48cl, 60cla; JPL - Caltech / University of Arizona 28br; JPL / Space Science Institute 29cra; JPL / University of Arizona 28ca, 29cb (Europa), 29cla, 29crb; JPL / USGS 8l, 29cb (Moon), 63bc, 63cr; Kennedy Space Center 23cra, 35tr, 38tl; MSFC 32cl, 33tr, 54-55c, 58bl, 59r, 70br, 70cla; National Geographic Society 32-33bc; NSSDC 3tr, 25cb, 25tr, 36tr, 37bc, 52cr, 62clb; NSSDC / USGS 52c; Project Apollo Archive 1, 4cla, 20b, 22tl, 23bl, 23cb, 23tc, 23tl, 24-25bc, 25br, 25ca, 35bl, 37br, 38cla, 39bl, 40bl, 40-41bc, 41cr, 41tl, 44cl, 44-45bc, 45cra, 45tc, 45tl, 46bl, 47bc, 47tl, 47tr, 50cl, 62bl, 63cra, 64-65 (Background), 65bl, 66-67 (Background), 68-69 (Background), 70-71 (Background) 47cr; Sean Smith 55cra; Image courtesy History of Science Collections, University of Oklahoma Libraries; copyright the Board of Regents of the University of Oklahoma: 67cl; PA Photos: Pat Sullivan 43br;

Photolibrary: Ian Paterson 68cl; Rex Features: Aldo Patellani 27tc; SNAP 33cr; Photo Scala, Florence: Biblioteca Nazionale, Florence 30cla; Courtesy of the Charles M. Schulz Museum and Research Center, Santa Rosa, California: 41tr; Science & Society Picture Library: 30bl, 31l; Science Photo Library: Jean-Loup Charmet 3tl, 12bl; Mark Garlick 18tl; Gary Hincks 22b; NASA 47tc; Pekka Parviainen 8cr, 9bl; Roger Ressmeyer 18bl; Ria Novosti 34br, 36cl, 37cr, 49bl, 49tl; after Selenotopographische Fragmente, 1791 by Johann Hieronymus Schröter 30bc; Still Pictures: Andia.fr / Godard 16-17b; Biosphoto / Vincent Decorde 11tl; SplashdownDirect / Michael Nolan 11br; USGS: 29br; Courtesy Virgin Galactic: 59bl; Werner Forman Archive: Sheldon Jackson Museum, Sitka, Alaska 2cb, 7tr.

Wall chart: Corbis: Roger Ressmeyer crb; DK Images: Courtesy of The Science Museum, London tl; iStockphoto.com: ca; NASA: br, cl, fbl; Johnson Space Center cb; Project Apollo Archives bl, cr, cra

Jacket images: Front: Corbis: Roger Ressmeyer tl; NASA: b. Back: Galaxy: Robin Scagell: tl; Rex Features: Snap: cl; Science and Society Picture Library: tr.

All other images © Dorling Kindersley
For further information see:
www.dkimages.com